ANCIENT PASSIONS

Produced by Raymond Creed,

Author of: -
- The 52 Attributes
- Facing the Unthinkable
- The Leeds Liturgy
- The Phantom Conflict

Storefront
http://stores.lulu.com/rebuildchristianity or
http://stores.lulu.com/store.php?fAcctID=976144

Editions available through Amazon and other International Book Distributors.

The cover photograph shows the bullet holes outside the Zion Gate of Jerusalem was taken by the author on Tuesday, 13th August 2019.

ANCIENT PASSIONS

(Exploring the Spiritual Crisis of Our Time)

Produced by Raymond Creed

Copyright © the Author 2018
(Backdated to cover all material produced by the author before 2018)

All Rights Reserved
The Moral Right of the author has been asserted

ISBN: 978-1-910871-91-1

CONTENTS

Glossary	XIII
Preface	XVI
Synopsis	XXX

PART A: ANCIENT HATRED   1

Introduction   3

Act 1: The Causes   5

Scene 1: The Haters   5
1. A Judas Kiss   5
2. Aquarian Era   6
3. Beslan   7
4. Bigotry   7
5. Bless You   8
6. Bombed out Church   9
7. Entanglements   11
8. God Is Not Happy   13
9. Old Horror   14
10. National Degeneracy   16
11. Prince of Terror   20
12. Three Brothers   21
    End Notes: 22

Scene 2: The Faithless   23
1. Anger   23
2. Church of Satan   23
3. House of Darkness   27
4. How I Grieve   28
5. Keep Faithful   29
6. Leaving   31
7. Settling for Decline   31
8. Stand-Up   33
9. Stones   34
10. The Wall   35
11. Truth   36
12. Turn   37
    End Notes: 38

Act 2: The Corruption 40

Scene 1: The Apostates 40
    1. Broken Churches 40
    2. Business as Usual 45
    3. Complicity 47
    4. Compromise 48
    5. Dedicated Follower 49
    6. Failure 52
    7. Fountain of Life 52
    8. How Did It End Like This? 53
    9. In Reality 53
    10. Lament for a Lost Friend 54
    11. Monochrome 57
    12. My Lady 58
    13. Roll-up: See the Gospel Circus Show 59
    14. So Much 62
    15. Taking Leave 64
    16. The Parable of the Drunkard 67
    17. Year after Year 67
    End Notes 68

Scene 2: Mother and Daughter 70
The Mother 70
    1. Alas 70
    1. Bloody Irony 71
    2. Depart from Me 71
    3. Disapproving Gaze 74
    4. Hide It 76
    5. Leering Skulls 77
    6. Loathing 79
    7. Prissy Priest 81
    8. Proud Rome 83
    9. Shaking Off 84
    10. Touching the Foot 85
    End Notes: 86
The Daughter 87
    1. Anglican Agony 87
    2. Bishop of Sin 88
    3. How Dare They? 91
    4. How Many 94

5.	New Age Woman	94
6.	Ritual Defilement	96
7.	Small Ambitions	98
8.	The Answer	99
9.	The Stroke of a Pen	101
10.	Unity	102
11.	Unleashed	103
12.	What Madness	107
13.	Withdrawal	108
14.	You Were	110
	End Notes:	114

Act 3: The Catastrophe — 116

Scene 1: The Wastelands — 116

1.	A Plea for Deliverance	116
2.	Memorial Cities	117
3.	Nuclear Sorrows	121
4.	Preserve Us	122
5.	Seeing	123
6.	Storm Warning	124
7.	The Abortion of Hope	125
8.	The Nations Hiss	131
	End Notes:	132

Scene 2: The Survivors — 133

1.	Defeated	133
2.	Fill	134
3.	Fog	134
4.	Legacy	134
5.	Pride	135
6.	Relating to Jesus	135
7.	Relief	135
8.	Stand Still	136
9.	Sweep In	136
10.	They Promised	137
11.	Vulnerability	145
12.	What Hope?	147
13.	Young Man	147
	End Notes:	148

Act 4: The Crisis — 150

Scene 1: The Great Delusion — 150
  1. A New Age — 150
  2. Deceiver — 151
  3. Global Messiah — 152
  4. Gnostic Christ — 154
  5. May I Not See — 158
  6. Misleading Advice — 158
  7. Relax — 159
  8. Solstice Twilight — 160
  9. The Seeking — 163
  10. They Do Not See — 164
  11. Why Waste time? — 165
  End Notes: — 166

Scene 2: The Martyrs — 168
  1. Are You Willing? — 168
  2. Bring — 169
  3. Illumination — 169
  4. Last Thoughts — 169
  5. My Lord Jesus Christ — 170
  6. Persecution — 172
  7. Please Remember — 173
  8. Priorities — 174
  9. Send — 174
  10. The Leading — 175
  11. The Martyr's Prayer — 175
  12. The Spirit Calls — 176
  13. Trust — 177
  14. When — 177
  End Notes: — 179

PART B: ANCIENT LOVE — 181

Introduction — 183

Act 5: The Cross — 185

Scene 1: The Sacrifice — 185
  1. Believe On! — 185
  2. Blood Flood — 188

3.	First and Final Hope	188
4.	Give Glory	189
5.	If You	191
6.	Joy	192
7.	Let Love	193
8.	Love Not	194
9.	Oh Jesus!	195
10.	Sin Bin	196
11.	The Way	198
12.	This is the Death	199
13.	Wave upon Wave	200
End Notes:		**202**

Scene 2: The Forgiven **203**

1.	Awesome Grace	203
2.	Dear Jesus!	204
3.	Confidence	204
4.	Firmly Moored	204
5.	For my Sin	205
6.	Grace and Mercy	205
7.	Gratitude	206
8.	Open	206
9.	Priority	207
10.	Soaking	207
11.	Thanksgiving	207
12.	The Poor Man	208
End Notes:		**209**

Act 6: The Calling 210

Scene 1: The Commissioning **210**

1.	Carry On	210
2.	Cascade	211
3.	Commissioned	212
4.	Discourse	214
5.	Faith	214
6.	Fear Not	215
7.	Follow	216
8.	Glad Surrender	217
9.	Grandson	219
10.	Let Me Run	219
11.	Motive	220

12.	Sent	220
13.	Serve	221
14.	The Charger	222
15.	Through	223
16.	Why Me?	224
	End Notes:	**225**

Scene 2: The Testimony — 227

1.	A Cry for Deliverance	227
2.	Babylon	228
3.	Bit-by-Bit	229
4.	Cloud Watching	229
5.	Conviction of Sin	230
6.	Desires	231
7.	Detesting	232
8.	Drastic Means	232
9.	God Is My Guide – Why Worry?	233
10.	Have I Been Wrong?	234
11.	How Long?	235
12.	I Seek	236
13.	In Monastery Gardens	236
14.	In Quiet Confidence	237
15.	It Was Through Mercy	238
16.	Let Down: A Writer's Lament	239
17.	Progression	242
18.	Pruning	243
19.	Revelation at the Door	244
20.	The Devoted	245
	End Notes:	**246**

Act 7: The Coming — 249

Scene 1: The Judgement — 249

1.	Accursed	249
2.	Anguish	250
3.	Calamity	251
4.	From Dust to Life	252
5.	Good and Evil	266
6.	H12	267
7.	How Lost	268
8.	Ours was the Folly	269
9.	What Good?	271

	End Notes:	273

Scene 2: The Deliverance **274**
    1. Answered 274
    2. By His Power 275
    3. Cravings 276
    4. Faithful Witness 277
    5. Old Time Gospel Plea 277
    6. Only Jesus Can 279
    7. No One 279
    8. Vindication 280
    9. What Beginning Is This? 281
    End Notes: **282**

Act 8: Completion 283

Scene 1: The Celebration **283**
    1. Appreciation 284
    2. Blessed 285
    3. Bond of Love 286
    4. Bountiful Mercy 286
    5. Breezy Delight 286
    6. By 287
    7. Celebrate 287
    8. Enraptured 289
    9. Even Closer 290
    10. Exalt 290
    11. Let Silence be my Song 291
    12. Let us praise Him 292
    13. One Lord 293
    14. Praise You 294
    15. Seeing You 294
    16. To Lofty Heights 295
    End Notes: **295**

Scene 2: The Lord of All **297**
    1. All Praise 297
    2. Behold 297
    3. Come – Go In 298
    4. Elohim 298
    5. Families 299
    6. How Great 300

7.	In the Stillness	300
8.	It Bestows	301
9.	Life and death	304
10.	My Heart	305
11.	Presence	306
12.	Rejoice	311
13.	The Beauty of the Lord	311
14.	The God of Holy Love	312
15.	Trinity	314
16.	Triune Worship	314
17.	Wonderful Blessing	315
18.	Postscript Guard Your heart	317
End Notes:		**319**

Selective Bibliography 321

Booklist 321
Media Sources 321

Other Titles by the Author 323

The 52 Attributes of God 325
Facing the Unthinkable 326
The Leeds Liturgy 327
The Phantom Conflict 328

Notes 330

GLOSSARY

Ancient: Something originating from (or belonging to) a bygone age – in the far distant past.

Ancient Passion: A passion, having originated in the far distant past (or in God's case – from eternity) but capable of strongly affecting present-day behaviour.

Apostasy: A wilful *'turning aside'* from the Gospel of Jesus Christ and from the teaching of His Word (the Bible).

Passion: A strong and (at times) overwhelming emotion, feeling or urge – capable of motivating very constructive (as well as very destructive) behaviour.

Christians: A person who claims to believe in, follow or represent Jesus Christ. This designation may be used in its narrower sense to refer to a *'regenerate believer'* – one who enjoys an actual personal relationship with God through his/her faith in Jesus Christ. It is used interchangeably with *'believer'* or *'follower of Christ.'*

Church: Used in its broadest sense, it refers to any Group, Organisation or Tradition claiming to represent the Lord Jesus Christ. It may be used interchangeably with the word *'Christianity'* or employed as an abbreviated version of *'the Global Church'* or *'Global Christianity.'* Obviously, it's debatable whether <u>all</u> churches are *'Christian'* in any meaningful biblical sense of the word.

Crisis: A sudden, possibly dangerous event (or series of events) which may pose a moral dilemma. Major decisions may need to be taken whilst under great pressure and tight time constraints. Types of *'Crises'* may include: -
- **A Slow Acting Crisis:** where a situation has not been dealt with in its initial stages. Problems and situations have been neglected and left to worsen over time. One historical example was the failure to have had proper fire regulations put in place in a crowded city like mid-eighteenth-century Lisbon, the (then wealthy) capital of Portugal. This situation

resulted in major fires following the severe earthquake which struck Lisbon on Saturday, 1st November 1755.

- **A Sudden Crisis:** where a situation appears unexpectedly from nowhere (what insurance companies call *'an act of God.'*) One example was the previously mentioned earthquake in Lisbon.

- **A *'Hybrid'* Crisis:** combining elements from each of the above terms – as evidenced when the Lisbon earthquake was immediately followed by a series of tsunamis and a terrible firestorm.

- **A Spiritual Crisis:** this forces a choice between a truth and a lie. In essence, it's a choice between God and Satan or Christ and anti-Christ. As such, it may decide one's eternal destiny. A major spiritual crisis usually occurs when the Cosmic war between God and Satan is particularly intense. One example was the conflict experienced by the *'Early Church'* when it needed to choose between true Apostolic and false Gnostic representations of Christ.

Magical Thinking: An extreme form of subjective thinking based upon the belief that people can *'magically'* create their own reality. Little or no regard is given to external constraints or possible negative consequences. It denies any form of objective reality.

Midrash: The Jewish method of interpreting scripture – as used by Jesus and the Apostles. The word *'Midrash'* derives from the Hebrew word *'Daresh'* meaning *'to make a rigorous investigation of.'*

Mysticism: A complex network of religious beliefs and devotional practices. It seek to initiate its devotees into mysterious spiritual *'secrets,'* *'special knowledge'* or *'higher truths,'* viewed as being unattainable by the average person. Possessing a chameleon-like quality, mysticism tends to manifest itself in all Christian and non-Christian belief systems.

Mystic: A committed practitioner of mysticism – one ardently seeking out and receiving (often untested) religious experiences – e.g. an angelic revelation. These may have been apparent in childhood (representing an inherited condition known as a *'bloodline'*). Alternatively, they may have resulted from a particular pagan *'initiation ceremony.'*

Objective Reality (or Truth): Anything that continues to exist, regardless of human perception or belief. Such a reality may either be accessible through the human senses or require systematic scientific investigation. An example of the latter was the discovery of sub-atomic particles like the Higgs Bosom.

Rational Thinking: A logical type of thinking aimed at a better understanding of objective reality. It may employs evidence, reason and scientific procedures to advance human.

Spiritual Warfare: The unremitting struggle between God and Satan, waged in the spiritual and earthly spheres. God is represented by His angels and Satan by his demons (the latter seeking to seduce human beings into following his evil ways). Scripture teaches that God is the ultimate victor in this conflict. (Somewhat confusingly, it has also been termed as the **Cosmic War,** thereby giving the misleading impression of fighting space monsters!)

Spirituality: Referring to anything pertaining to the *'spiritual often realm'* or *'human soul,'* often undervaluing the material or physical realms. (It is used interchangeably with the word *'Mysticism.'*)

Subjective Thinking: A type of thinking based upon experienced emotion and the belief that we can create and live in our own perceived, truth regardless of external reality.

PREFACE

Creative Pieces

Ancient Passions is a collection of lively, creative and meditative pieces, written over a span of almost forty-four years (1975-2020). It reflects those inner psychological and spiritual motivations directly governing human behaviour. These (often complex) motivations interact continuously with the external environment, generating passions that influence (for better or worse) the world around us.

Each society is a product of human passion. Whole civilizations have been created (or destroyed) by the deeply felt hatreds (or loves) which once dominated them. As the financial crisis of September 2008 and the US Presidential election of 2016 demonstrated, human passion really does influence the economic and political behaviour of whole nations. Another example are the many (passionately felt) hatreds of the Middle East. Such fervent human passions could set in motion a whole train of events, leading eventually to the deaths of millions (as portrayed in the spine-chilling scenario of *Memorial Cities*). The world appears to be succumbing to a type of *'hyper-irrationality'* which may well lead to an increase in lawlessness and a greater proclivity to follow a charismatic *'Global Deliverer.'* Once *'human'* reasoning is rejected people become open to anything – especially so in the throes of a major, life-threatening crisis. This very scenario is what Climate Change (with its resultant environmental disasters) could well bring about on a truly gargantuan scale.

Lending Credibility

Ancient Passions portrays the whole of humanity as teetering on the edge of a multi-dimensional, all-encompassing crisis. Those areas touching upon human life, *e.g.* the political, economic, social, technological, environmental and legal, will all be affected. This crisis will develop in response to a whole series of (often traumatic) events where people will have had to choose between the truth (as revealed in scripture) or an enticing worldwide lie

XVII

(appealing to their deepest desires). The severity and intensity of these events will have created the sort of fear and desperation that looks for scapegoats and heightens receptivity to some kind of global saviour. Even now (2020) current world developments lend credibility to the scenario of a coming anti-Christ (as portrayed in **Revelation 13-14.**) A spiritual crisis (forcing people to choose between Christ and the anti-Christ) will be another aspect of this multi-dimensional crisis.

In once *'tolerant'* countries (like the UK or USA) Christians are beginning to endure the political and social marginalization which often precedes outright oppression. This is borne out by the number of cases where Christians have been dismissed from their jobs, had their businesses closed through boycotts or have faced legal action following a traditional stand on same-sex marriage. Belief in *'liberty of personal conscience'* appears to be dying in Western Culture. Coming into its place is an increasingly coercive, state-based authoritarianism.

Christians all across the world are set to face a choice between conforming to an evil system of government (demanding absolute loyalty) or resisting it by boldly confessing their faith – thereby inviting persecution and possibly martyrdom. This was precisely the choice faced by the early Christians in the Roman Empire – and which still exists today in places like North Korea.

This book confirms that I have little time for the established, organizational forms of Christianity (or what I call *'pseudoanity.'*) The latter are even now thundering down the road to Global Apostasy and worship of the anti-Christ. Church leaders will betray their flocks and prioritise *'social acceptability'* above all else. Many in their congregations will be shocked at the speed and extent of this betrayal. However, balancing this pessimistic picture is the confidence that Christ will guard those who are truly His – for God's mercy will appear in all sorts of unexpected places and amongst the most unlikely of people.

XVIII

A Telling Contrast

Human passion can either be a wonderfully creative or is horribly destructive thing. This point is readily seen in any visit made to the Sistine Chapel in the Vatican. There, a passion to create, displayed by artists such as Michelangelo (1475-1564) produced some of the most beautiful artworks in the world. Yet also present was a dark passion for power shown by successive popes whose high-handed arrogance provoked the Reformation and successive wars of religion. This one geographical location displayed the best – and worst of human passions.

However, a world without passion would be a world without art, science or emotional warmth – with people being little better than the brute beasts. Passion is therefore essential for human survival; it's that which defines us as human beings. Conversely, a world full of destructive passion alone would be Hell itself – with nothing but continual warfare. As a human quality *'passion'* is essential – yet sadly <u>always</u> having the potential to be extremely dangerous. It constantly needs to be channelled into sound and creative outlets – after all, it is so much a part of our world.

A reading of scripture would indicate that human passion is at once both noble and yet flawed. As human beings we have been made in the image of God **(Genesis 1:26).** This is reflected in the noble, beneficent and loving passions that contribute to so much social progress. Sadly, we are also *'fallen sinners'* who all too willingly indulge in the baser aspects of human nature (*i.e.* anger, fear, hatred and self-centeredness). Man is in constant rebellion against God and is easily seduced by demonic forces, **(Mark 5:1-20).** Both aspects *i.e. 'saintly man'* (made in the image of God) and *'selfish man'* (casually following the ways of Satan) can be present in one and the same person and at more-or-less the same time. Both Stalin and Mao were fine poets with a real feeling for language but were also the biggest mass murderers of their day. Being *'cultured'* <u>does not,</u> and <u>never has</u> guaranteed immunity from evil. On the contrary, a high level of culture may afford the evildoer much more scope to inflict a greater amount of harm.

However, scripture also shows us that human history consists of far more than just an interaction of human passion with its external environment. In essence, it always has been – and still is – more a case of human passion <u>interacting with</u> divine passion <u>and</u> with the destructive passions of Satan. (The latter is constantly governed by an unreasoning hatred which seeks to spoil or destroy God's handiworks). Divine passion seeks to build-up love **(1 John 4:8)** whilst diabolical passion always seeks to stir up hatred. One gives life and creativity, whilst the other seeks to *'kill and to destroy'* **(John 8:44).** If divine passion is *'all good'* and diabolical passion *'all bad'* then human passion is a mixture of both. This means that the interplay between divine, human and diabolic passion can be likened to single colours – all vigorously being stirred together until no single discernible colour remains. All *'passions'* are *'in the mix.'* Such is the complexity of human life and feeling.

In passing, it's worth stating that (sin wrecked) human passion contrasts vividly with divine passion – the latter most clearly expressed in the life and work of Jesus Christ. Divine passion is always perfectly controlled (as seen in Christ's enormous self-restraint during His Crucifixion – considered to be one of the most degrading of punishments in the Roman Empire.) In contrast, human passion is often self-centred, volatile and uncontrolled.

Ancient Passions has deliberately shunned the Platonic World View (which assumes that God is a deity devoid of passion and largely unmoved by the affairs of His Creation.) The scriptural (and more accurate) representation of God sees Him as a Father, able to feel incredibly strong passions, yet always in control due to His great wisdom. In addition, He is completely free from any trace of selfishness and impurity. Furthermore, God's passion is abundantly creative, manifesting itself in a whole multitude of ways. This can be seen in the zeal Jesus frequently demonstrated during the course of His earthly Ministry. His ability to experience emotion equips Him to relate closely (and even personally identify) with His Creation and to empathise with us. He can feel our rawest emotions. This present work seeks to correct the dry (Platonic) intellectual approach of the past – replacing it with the sure (and scriptural) knowledge of someone who is deeply caring and totally involved in human affairs. The Deity whom Christians follow is an emotionally committed God.

Structure

In terms of structure, **Ancient Passions** is divided into two halves: **Part A** and **Part B**. It is then further sub-divided into **four** *'Acts,'* each consisting of **two** dramatic *'Scenes,'* deliberately placed to bring the narrative to life. A definite progression is made from the negative themes explored in **Part A** to the more positive aspects of **Part B**.

Part A examines the chilling reality of human and satanic rebellion against God. Highlighted is the grim fact that, in the Western World especially, we live in an age of mass apostasy. This state of affairs is already harmfully affecting the wider culture where potentially violent forms of political and religious extremism are on the rise in many places throughout the world. At senior levels, some denominations (like the Church of England and Methodism) are abandoning any pretence of following even the most moderate versions of traditional Christianity. Their leaders continue to foolishly conform to the dictates of an increasingly depraved culture. They have no confidence in Christ – as seen in their pronouncements and daily decisions. As a whole, the churches in the West give the impression of being run by ecclesiastical politicians rather than by committed followers of the risen Christ.

In contrast to **Part A, Part B** strikes a more positive and optimistic note. God's gracious rescue from the effects of Humanity's rebellion comes sharply into relief. Readers have firstly (in **Part A**) been taken to the hellish depths of human (and satanic) depravity before being lifted (in **Part B**) to an ecstatic worship of the one true God. As the book follows the plotline of scripture, the dark tone and content of **Part A** gives way to the lightness and victory in the last Act of **Part B**. Human sin reaches a terrible climax of evil under the instigation of a false global messiah before being overwhelmingly resolved by the sudden return of Jesus Christ. At this present time (2020), the impression remains that Humanity is being strategically prepared by Satan to

XXI

worship this chilling future figure. Moreover, the reign of this false messiah is set to have such catastrophic consequences that direct divine intervention will be the only answer to rescue humanity from its own (self-inflicted) extinction, **(Matthew 24:22)**.

One indication that Humanity is being *'programmed'* into accepting *'the anti-Christ'* is the way highly subjective (even magical) forms of thought is becoming predominant across the world. The latter rightly assumed there was some objective truth existing outside of ourselves. Now it seems that the younger generation readily *'construct'* their own reality or *'version of truth.'* (This is a feature on many Conspiracy Theory Websites.) When it comes to daily living, people make-up things as they go along. The inhabitants of what now passes for Western Civilization are increasingly losing their ability to think ever more rationally. Rulers (and ruled alike) are prone to delusory thinking and *'quick fixes'* that tend only to make a given problem worse.

Since the mid-1960s, a societal insanity has been steadily growing with the potential to consume millions of lives and produce horrors to rival that produced by Communism and Nazism the twentieth century.[1] Present is a sad contrast to the old, once rational way of thinking which respected carefully established facts, evidence-based reasoning and belief in the existence of objective truths. All of these mores were once accepted and steadily conformed to for the sake of humanity's well-being. It was this rational way of thinking that allowed the West to progress in the way it did.

Following Scripture

Ancient Passions traces the unfolding of human history. Its follows on from the biblical authors who recorded the re-occurring patterns (and bitter consequences) of sinful human behaviour. The same dynamics (of rebellion and deception) are to be found in any historical age. Sin is sin, no matter whether it's the sin of Adam or the sin of some future anti-

---

[1] This theme is thoroughly explored in my earlier book, *'Hoofbeats of the Apocalypse'* published under the pen name of Leo Arland.

XXII

Christ and the billions who will be seduced by him. The only difference is one of scale. What Satan did to Adam in the Garden of Eden will be done to the whole of the human race through his servant – the anti-Christ. There will be exactly the same appeal to pride, the same offer to *'become like God'* and the same spurious promise of a materially rich life. The end of human history is likely to see a replay of the scenario recounted in **Genesis 3,** only this time a global *'fall from grace'* is likely to lead to a worldwide destruction of the environment. Man, under Satan's grip, will ravage the whole Earth.

The presence (throughout history) of re-occurring patterns of human behaviour makes it possible to generalise from the smaller to the larger (even global) scenario. Hence, the neo-pagan superstitions of Roman Catholicism,[2] and the near-moribund disarray found within Anglicanism today can each be used to understand the process of apostasy. They may well be a *'dress rehearsal'* for the future *worldwide* apostasy of Christianity. This global event will, in each instance display the same casual compromise with evil, blind conformity and moral depravity and acceptance of idolatrous practices. Also, it will not confine itself to these traditions alone but will spill out to affect every single denomination throughout the whole of Christendom. Creative pieces such as *'Compromise'* and *'Roll-up'* (each referring to the Evangelical and Charismatic Pentecostal sectors of Christianity) confirm that apostasy is not a uniquely Roman Catholic or Anglican phenomena. Most Western Churches have already fallen *'out of love'* with Jesus Christ, **(Revelation 3:4-5).** For them, He is a convenient figurehead – there to justify essentially self-interested agendas such as trying to gain or maintain an influential social position.

For dramatic purposes the biblical scenario of *'The Last Days'* has been simplified. No mention is made of *'the rapture.*[3] Any

---

[2] Any misgivings that I'd overdramatized the corruption in Roman Catholicism were cured by a reading of Martel (2019). His excellent, well-documented book narrated forms of depraved behaviour that went even beyond my imagination!

[3] This is the belief that Christ will come secretly to *'snatch away'* His people shortly before His bodily return to this earth. He will do this in order to

XXIII

real events (which would normally be widely separated in time) are telescoped together.[4] Also, not every single biblical doctrine is covered – with some bible teachings (like the beauty of divine creation) being given only a passing mention.[5] Inevitably, some readers may feel aggrieved at this omission but to try and cover everything would be to destroy the very essence of this book. It's steady focus is upon <u>presenting those truths that need to be heard in our present day and age.</u>[6]

Connecting Events

The scriptural approach to human history is <u>capable of connecting apparently unrelated historical events.</u> For example, the popular enthusiasm surrounding the inauguration of President Barack Obama (in January 2009) could be seen as anticipating a similar (but more intense) enthusiasm accompanying the meteoric rise of a future Global Messiah. Such a figure will be carried to power on a wave of emotion. Certainly, the employment of Ancient Jewish methods of Bible Interpretation (called Midrash) has aided greatly in understanding the fascinating jumble of human history. <u>Midrash assumes that similar patterns of behaviour may re-occur in different historical epochs.</u>

A more contemporary note is struck regarding the viewpoints expressed in **Ancient Passions.** Readers will quickly notice that it jerks around as if it were a video camera, attempting to capture one scene here and then another there. In *'Deceiver'* a false prophet is seen as wanting glory for himself, whilst in

---

spare them the full horrors of the global judgments that will precede this return.

[4] **Revelation 20** would suggest that the final judgement of the unredeemed may occur one thousand years after Christ's return. For dramatic effect, I have portrayed this judgement as taking place immediately following Christ's return.

[5] It's not the intention to provide a detailed timetable of events surrounding the second coming of Christ. Doing so would impose an artificial rigidity upon the book's more poetical structure. It would inadvertently change a largely poetical work into a theological textbook, thereby defeating its purpose.

[6] Readers requiring a more balanced and comprehensive presentation of biblical teaching will find it in the Creedal Statements my prayer book, *'The Leeds Liturgy.'* This provides a precise outline of exactly what, and in whom, I believe. Precision and clarity are foremost in this work.

XXIV

'Memorial Cities' a cold-hearted bureaucrat is loyally serving the New World Order. Yet another switch and we have the *'The Martyr's Prayer'* where a faithful Christian believer is about to be slain by that very same *'New World Order.'* One of the major challenges when writing **Ancient Passions** was that of gaining greater insight into a particular individual *'mentality,'* no matter how repulsive it may have been. For example, getting into the mindset of *'The Gnostic Christ'* was no easy task. Yet, I felt it was an unpleasant job which needed to be done, so I persisted. Thankfully, I felt a curious sense of detachment when writing that piece. Psychologically, it had been necessary to separate myself from the character I was writing about.

A jerky quality also surfaces regarding the passage of time. Some creative items like *'You Were'* follow a simple linear sequence – where the past, present and future of the Church of England is summed-up in the form of a funeral epitaph. Others have a greater ambiguity *i.e.* is a meditation like *'Triune Worship'* located in the *'here and now'* or in some future afterlife? Here, the example of the Old Testament Prophets was most helpful. These sages' words would often simultaneously point to any number of things and events. One example such as the first and second coming of Christ, which in reality are widely separated in space and time. **Ancient Passions** likewise tends to portray repeated prophetic fulfilments (sometimes separated by long time intervals) as being telescoped together – all taking place in rapid succession.

Another approach (also gleaned from the Old Testament Prophets) was how they personally interacted with the truths they proclaimed – as seen in the *'confessions of Jeremiah,'* **(Jeremiah 12:1-13, 15:15f, 18:13f & 20:7f)**. This same approach is portrayed in the more autobiographical pieces like *'Fog.'* Akin to Jeremiah, I've also been near to despair, almost to the point of giving up – especially in relation to the demise of an established priestly religion (in my own case – the Church of England). I too have walked on the *'dark side of faith'* and been enticed by the errors of my own place and time. An unhealthy fanaticism on my part was a real temptation – especially in my younger Pentecostal days. But for the mercy of Jesus and the good influence of my dear late father I could easily have ended-up like the unpleasant character portrayed in *'Bigotry.'* One thing that knowing Jesus does do is to bring to light the more warped aspects of our own personality. His light exposes our inner darkness – but thankfully brings a measure of humility.

By this stage, it should be clear that I'm someone *'caught-up in'* and *'interacting with'* the complexity of contemporary human society. I'm not some *'loftier than thou'* critic, pontificating from the side-lines or from a monkish cell. Where possible, I've tried to engage with my surrounding society and culture, largely through my teaching profession and my participation in different cultural activities *e.g.* poetry evenings.

Biblical teaching methods and literary forms have been used throughout this work.⁷ God's Word is certainly a source of truth in and of itself. However, it is also the actual source of the teaching methods and literary forms used to convey that truth. Using these has greatly clarified the meaning of any pertinent scriptural text.

A variety of poetical forms have been taken from non-biblical cultures (with Japanese Haikus being a particular favourite). My poem, *'Aquarian Age'* brings this out very well, presenting (in Haiku form) a very biblical view of human affairs. This example confirms that I'm more than happy to appropriate non-biblical forms of poetry and fill them with biblical content.

Despite the use of non-biblical literary forms, my world view is derived mainly from scripture. It's often at serious odds with the atheistic, mystical, neo-pagan world views currently dominant throughout Western Civilization. In terms of outlook I have very little in common with most of my non-Christian contemporaries. This is because our value systems are completely different. Spiritually, we are veering off in two opposite directions. There really can be no accommodation between Christianity and the Totalitarian Ideologies of fallen

---

⁷ These include the use of parables and parallelisms – where the same point is made twice in one verse, but with slightly different words.

humanity. This is because, quite simply, they operate under two mutually antagonistic spiritual influences. Consequently, any attempt by Christians to gain social acceptability by *'diluting'* or *'accommodating'* their faith is bound to fail. The Spirit of Christ cannot mix with the spirit of anti-Christ. (This was a point the Apostle John repeatedly made in his first Epistle.)

An Important Caution

As a note of caution, it's perhaps wise to mention that **Ancient Passions** is primarily a work of poetry and <u>not</u> of prophecy. It was never intended as *'The Book of Revelation, Part Two!*[8] The same cautionary note is sounded should the reader look at my material for some esoteric meaning or special insight into future world developments. It really is best to view this work in a *'it means what it says'* fashion – unless it appears utterly nonsensical to do so. However, should any predictions within its pages come to pass <u>they would be as a direct result of having followed the scenario already laid down in scripture.</u> I have no special *'esoteric ability'* to divine what's to come. Everything to know concerning the future is to be found within scripture and it's to this source alone that people should turn to satisfy their curiosity. The poems and other material found in **Ancient Passions** simply re-affirm what scripture teaches and predicts. <u>I have knowingly revived biblical literary forms but have not promoted any new prophecy or hitherto unrevealed truth.</u> The nearest I've come to the prophetic side of things has been when describing my experience of God in prayer or recording an exhortation given in a local congregation decades ago. Such experiences can happen to any believer – there's nothing unique or *'extra biblical'* about them. In essence, this work offers an imaginative reiteration of biblical teaching and experience. Should the reader feel uncomfortable with its contents then they need only search out scripture to gauge whether **Ancient Passions** is in accord with God's Word, **(Acts 17:11).**

---

[8] If it has affinities with an early Christian work it is with the second century *'Shepherd of Hermas.'*

XXVII

Depths and Heights

Akin to the Medieval Italian Author, Dante Alighieri (1265-1321) in his poetical masterpiece *'The Divine Comedy'* I firstly cast readers into the infernal depths of Hell before raising them to the joyful heights of Heaven. However, there is a difference. In contrast to Dante, I highlight humanity's endless capacity to create a hell for itself right here on earth. This point needs to be urgently emphasised to this generation – which appears to have little (or no) knowledge of the devastation wrought by the totalitarian ideologies of the twentieth century. Sadly (and very worryingly) many members of this younger generation are often simply too immersed in computer games or the social media to have time to think for themselves or to learn from the past. I'm thankful that my own youth took place long before such distractions existed.

My own approach of *'first show them hell and then show them heaven'* is one having often been followed by both Catholic and Protestant Tradition. There's nothing new or outlandish about it – indeed Baptist ancestors of mine would have been very familiar with this particular way of doing things. Another example is that of the Salvation Army Founder William Booth (1829-1912) who, from the pulpit, was reputed to have *'dangled'* his hearers over the pit before announcing the wonderful news of Salvation in Jesus Christ! There is (in **Ancient Passions**) plenty of *'pit dangling!'* <u>To appreciate the light of Christ we must first become aware of the darkness in our own sinful nature and in the world around us.</u>

This book's stark approach challenges that type of theology which overemphasise divine love to the neglect of other (equally important) divine attributes, *e.g.* divine holiness or wrath. The *'all is love'* type of theology is unable to cope with tragedy or the kind of circumstances described in **Ancient Passions.** Unfortunately, this overemphasis upon love dominates most Churches in the Western World today. Those who have succumbed to it will find the contents of this work most disconcerting. (A comprehensive discussion of the weaknesses of the *'love alone'* approach will be found in Chapter 1: Section 5 of my work, entitled *'The Phantom Conflict.'*)

XXVIII

What is <u>not</u> on offer in **Ancient Passions** is the kind of *'Cheap Grace'* rightly criticised by the German Christian thinker and martyr, Dietrich Bonhoeffer (1906-1945). Simply stated, all that *'Cheap Grace'* says is *'come as you are and stay as you are.'* It offers a *'comfortable featherbed'* for sinners to doze upon. Instead, **Ancient Passions** returns to the approach followed by the late first century Christian Document *'The Didache'* which stressed that there are only two paths in life; one is a way of darkness – leading to eternal misery and the other a way of light – leading to eternal joy and friendship with Christ. Personally, I believe the apostasy now clearly apparent throughout Western Christianity has reached such a level that the approach followed by *'The Didache'* needs once again to be re-affirmed. <u>It is very much a case of displaying *'tough love'* when telling the truth.</u> The growing spiritual crisis of our time allows for no other approach. Being half-hearted or apologetic for the truth of the Gospel is rapidly ceasing to be a viable option for everyday Christians. We need to regain the boldness of our ancestors who witnessed fearlessly to the Gospel with little regard for their own personal popularity.

A Vigorous Presentation

What this work <u>does do is to offer a clear and vigorous presentation of the Gospel of Jesus Christ.</u> Indeed, the exhortation *'Believe On!'* is one such rousing proclamation, challenging readers to come to Jesus and receive His salvation. **Ancient Passions** ends on a thoroughly gospel-centred note. It reaches out (with the Gospel Message) in as creative and imaginative a manner as is possible. The author is only too aware that Western Culture is living in a post-Christian age, characterised by a horrendous increase in delusory thinking.

My aim has always been to portray the Lord Jesus Christ as someone full of a passionate but (wisely directed) loving holiness. This reflects the correct scriptural view of God – in total contrast to Him being regarded as a passive spectator or an indulgent *'sugar daddy.'* Also, firmly challenged is the erroneous view of Him as an impersonal Being – *'cosmic force'* (complete with a *'light'* and a *'dark'* side).

The God portrayed here is the God of Israel and the Father of our Lord Jesus Christ – who came in the flesh to die for the sins of the World, **(John 1:16, 3:16 & 1 John 4:1-3).** Should **Ancient Passions** enable any reader to enter into a relationship with God then it will have performed an invaluable service. May all who read this work be both challenged and comforted by its contents. My hope is that in due time, it will become a *'classic'* of Christian spirituality.

The Author, March 2020

SYNOPSIS

Ancient Passions is a creative work employing a variety of literary forms to cover important aspects of the Christian life. It presents a variety of themes, including bible prophecy, corruption in the Church and the decline of Western Civilization. It emphasises God's enduring love for those who trust in Him.

Ancient Passions is divided into two parts: -
PART A explores grim themes like sin, judgement and the rise of anti-Christ. Emphasis is given to God's holiness and His wrath against sin.
PART B explores more joyful themes, including redemption, forgiveness, revival and the second coming of Christ. Emphasis is given to God's love and His mercy to sinners.

In both parts, Christ's death upon the cross is boldly proclaimed as being the <u>only</u> answer to human sinfulness.

This work warns against the growing madness of a culture where self-centredness and unreason increasingly underpin human behaviour. It explores the psychological and spiritual passions driving that madness.

It assumes that (in the not too distant future) the whole of humanity will face an immense worldwide spiritual crisis. Circumstances will force every adult person to choose between following the revealed truth of scripture or a highly attractive global deception, appearing to be *'truer than truth itself.'* The latter may be led by an extremely plausible, charismatic figure, with massive popular appeal (in Scripture known as *'The anti-Christ'*). The effect of his rule will be the near extinction of humanity, **(Matthew 24:22).**

God will ultimately triumph, but at present, He is restraining His power on earth in order to give human beings a chance to repent and turn to Him, **(2 Peter 3:9-10)**. In **Ancient Passions** readers are given a foretaste of Hell and then, thankfully, Heaven.

PART A: ANCIENT HATRED

(Church Apostasy and Humanity's Rebellion Against God)

2

INTRODUCTION

Ancient Hatred forms the first part of this creative and dramatic work. It consists of Four Acts each expressing the theme of human rebellion against God (and its destructive consequences). It portrays Humanity's increased vulnerability to satanic deception – in all its various forms. It assumes that the logical result of de-Christianisation is the mass extermination society where cruelty and murder become the norm.

A sequential relationship is embedded within that initial rebellion as shown here: -

Humanity's rebellion against God
⇓
Domination by sinful passions
⇓
The production of long-lasting hatreds
⇓
Faithlessness in the Church
⇓
Increased vulnerability to satanic deception
⇓
The development of an anti-Christian *'New World Order'*
⇓
The rise of a false Messiah to head that *'Order'*
⇓
The persecution of Jewish and Christian dissenters
⇓
Bitterly destructive consequences
⇓
The near-total destruction of Humanity

Readers will quickly gather from **Ancient Hatred** that the emphasis is upon the awful consequences of human sin. Humanity descends into its own man-made Hell, whilst the Church degenerates into a willing tool of the anti-Christ. Although shards of light emerge in meditations like *'The Spirit Calls'* it is the dark side of life which comes to the fore. God is portrayed as a wrathful Judge – allowing people to experience the bitter consequences of their rebellion against Him. The focus is upon Man's alienation from God – often hidden under the guise of religion. Portrayed in meditations like *'Lament for a Lost Friend'* and *'My Lady'* is the cost apostasy incurs in terms of broken relationships, moral scandal and emotional distress. Such pieces confirm that my approach to this problem is not as an *'ivory tower'* critic of the Church but an active participant. I too have been distressed by some of the situations described in this book. I wish to express how it felt to have lived through a period of mass apostasy and growing social madness. The focus here is upon the spiritual (rather than the cultural) dimension. Insight is given into the Spiritual War currently being waged between absolute good and absolute evil. Furthermore, it's a war that involves every Christian believer.

ACT 1: THE CAUSES

SCENE 1: THE HATERS

John 16:2, *"They shall put you out of the synagogues: the time will come when those who kill you will think that they are doing God a service."*

A JUDAS KISS

This is an age of Apostasy: -
An age where there's next to no faith here on earth
An age where church leaders cease to follow Jesus
An age where church members have *'itching ears for error'*
An age where falsehood abounds, and truth is despised
An age where each person pursues their own interests
Regardless of the cost to others
An age where the Gospel is silenced
And the way of salvation is deliberately forgotten

Truly, these are *'perilous times'*
Calling for endurance
By the few who know their Lord

Each person does *'what is right in their own eyes'*
Most are addicted to pleasure
Whilst a few are driven
By a fanatical intensity.
That's closed to reason

Mitred apostates in gaudy robes sit in council
Plotting to follow the One who deserves no name –
He who will bedazzle many with his promises
Only to wreak destruction across the earth
Truly, those who abandon Christ <u>will</u> follow an anti-Christ
This is their judgement

Weep and howl! The Church has abandoned God
Instead, it follows the destructive ideals of a rebellious world
Once more, Jesus has been betrayed by a Judas kiss

AQUARIAN ERA

An Aquarian era
Has rapidly dawned
It promises much
But a confused dismay lingers
For people no longer know
Who they are or what to do
With mad fervour they cling
To fabricated idols

Worshipping themselves with techno-aps
Irrationality rules OK
Reason has died
Only a bleak desperation remains

Suddenly ...

A new faith beckons
To ignite a fervent zeal
A charismatic saviour
Promises a 'New World Order'
Mass seduction follows in his wake
But his united "Global State"
Is founded on empty hopes
To trust in him is to be deluded
For all his promises are lies

Behold! A Master of deception
Terror reigns, persecution begins
Endurance is required by the faithful

Climate catastrophe
Mega storms rage
In a darkened sky
Overhung by a dim, blood red moon
Booms of thunder reverberate
Lightning bolts decimate
They flash and flicker
With garish intensity
Continents burn

Spinning tornados perform
A fiery dance of death
Amidst a choking, smoking gloom
Lost souls cry out in piteous anguish
Hell has come to Earth
Sing a requiem to our world

Global torment
Armies of blood arrayed against each other
Mass extinction beckons
A final *'last stand'* is taken by humanity

Who can save us now?

BESLAN

Many voices are heard in Beslan
"Lamentation and bitter weeping" (Jeremiah 31:15)
Many mothers weep for their children
Many fathers vow revenge
Shamefaced officials offer their apologies
For the children slain
By the Herods of this age

Where have the children gone?
They are lying in body bags
Slaughtered by those whose pitiless massacre
Was justified in the name of God

BIGOTRY

Death to America
Death to Israel
Death to the Jews
Death to the Arabs
Death to the *'Left'*
Death to the *'Right'*
Death to the ethnic minorities
Death to the sexual minorities
Death to all of <u>YOU</u>
Who don't submit to <u>my</u> views!

BLESS YOU

Bless you Eighteenth century philosophers for showing us that reason is <u>not</u> the solution to Man's problems

Bless you Karl Marx for showing us that injustice cannot be conquered by hatred

Bless you Vladimir Lenin for showing us that class war ends in futile destruction

Bless you Joseph Stalin for showing us that unlimited power brings no happiness

Bless you Chairman Mao for showing us that human nature is basically bad

Bless you all evil men of history for showing us that, without God's love, we are nothing

But then those from the past rise-up and loudly declare; *'You are alive and well, but we are the dead who were slain by those you have blessed!'*

BOMBED-OUT CHURCH

Hymns of praise
Now exchanged
For the groans of death
Joyous choruses
Now exchanged
For the gargling
Of those gasping for breath
Sweet scent of female perfume
Now exchanged
For the stench of discharging body fluids

The charred head of a suicide bomber
Grins malignantly from the rafters
Eyes closed in smug satisfaction

An arrogant Church
That idolized its tradition
Has been given over
To a terrible enemy -
One who laughs gleefully
At the suffering caused

Soon ...

Cities will blaze
And Civilizations crash.
A curse upon those fanatics
(Of any faith)
Who continue to deny
That murder in the name of God
Is blasphemy

A shrapnel-torn icon
Hangs uselessly
Unable to see, help or speak
Amidst a tumble of communion vessels
Church dignitaries lie dead
Sprawled around an altar
Their robes stained with blood.
An unbelieving minister

Who'd scorned Christ's Atonement
As a form of *'Cosmic Child abuse.'*
Clings helplessly to a broken crucifix
As his soul slips into
An unquenchable fire

Amidst the debris of upturned chairs
Under a fading, flickering light
The congregation lie on a cold stone floor
Like broken marionettes
Most lie silent
But some still convulse and shake
Just as they did
When receiving a spurious blessing from false prophets
Only now the curse is obvious.
Some call to a long-deceased parent
Whilst others wheeze inarticulate words
And curse a deity they'd never really believed in
Only a few will find peace in their last moments on Earth

Here or there
A prayer is made
To a non-responding God.

But …

No one warned them that a time of mercy
Was coming to an end.

No one warned them that the Lord's wrath
Was something to be feared.

No one warned them that Christ
Demanded complete allegiance.

Leaders lied and the people were lost!

The lights fail
And darkness closes in

ENTANGLEMENTS

How I grieve for the future of Israel
How I weep for what is to come

Her enemies have formed an unholy coalition
An alliance of evil has begun to emerge

They poison the media with their lies
They fill the airways with their slander

A serpentine conspiracy has been hatched
A protocol of hatred has been struck

Britain has become an addled Isle
With no capacity to resist evil

Her population seeks only pleasure
And its youth waste themselves on dissipation

The works of darkness are eagerly supported
Whilst moral standards are quickly subverted

Human rights laws bless unrighteousness
A legal haven is provided for iniquity

Even the best of leaders lack courage
Whilst the worst boldly support evil

Westminster politicians spread deceit like confetti
They are smooth practitioners of the *'honeyed lie'*

From top to bottom there is only corruption
And from head to toe a wasting decay

The churches have abandoned their mission
No truth is preached from the pulpit

The gospel of Christ has long been rejected
And the Word of Life spurned

Self-righteous leaders prattle about social justice
But theirs is a blind conformity to secular fashion

An old hatred has become socially acceptable
Open support is given to the violently wicked

Denominations agree to boycott Israeli goods
They have become complicit in a cruel genocide[9]

The teachings of *'Jesus the Jew'* are forsaken
The way of Christ is casually abandoned

The State of Israel now stands alone
She is a scapegoat among the nations

Those who wish to destroy her mobilise their resources
Those who seek her annihilation gather together

But in Britain the public look on with sleepy indifference
Unmoved and uncaring about the destruction of the Jews –
Instead they press the TV remote
Or switch to another social media site

Oh, you who claim to belong to *'the faithful remnant'*
Wake up! Stir yourselves!
Repent of your apathy!
And get on with praying
Ask Yahweh to remember His covenant promises
Beg Him to recall His promises made to Abraham
Cry out that He must keep His Word
That Israel will <u>not</u> be destroyed!
That His people will, once more, know the Lord

---

[9] A reference to a key decision (made at the July 2010 Methodist Conference) to accept a report calling for the boycott of Israeli goods from the West Bank area

GOD IS NOT HAPPY

God is not made happy
By those who kill and maim in His name
He is no Morloch
Demanding endless human sacrifices
To appease His wrath

Nor is He a devil
Hungering after the sacrifice of children
To satiate His need for total worship

Those who kill in His name
Will be flung into hell
Those who incite children to kill in His name
Will be flung into the deepest part of hell

Once there
They will be accused by those whom they misled
For all of eternity

OLD HORROR

A horror from of old
A horror from the recesses of Hell
A horror springing from corrupt human hearts
It is the horror of anti-Semitism
Many are its lies and deceits

It will bring
Distress and tribulation
Ruin and devastation
Darkness and gloom (Zephaniah 1:15-16)

It will express itself
In the poisonous gas cloud
The looming mushroom cloud
The nuclear blast and shock wave

This horror cannot be
Contained
Appeased
Nor reasoned with

For it seeks the annihilation of Israel
It plots the destruction of the Jews
It yearns to make an end of Zion

Behold!
A coalition of evil begins to form
An alliance of killers comes into being
A well-armed confederacy assaults the land
Its members wish to destroy a Covenant People

Then the Lord remembers His promises to Abraham
He recalls His covenant with David
And listens to the pleadings of His great High Priest

He looks on with disgust
He snorts with fury
He unsheathes His sword of judgement

The alliance of evil arrogantly advances
Slaying all who stand in its way
The wicked gloat openly at its progress
The world looks on with alarm and yet achieves nothing
Diplomatic pleas are contemptuously ignored (Ezekiel 38:13)

'A Final Solution to the Jewish Question' appears inevitable
The hopes of generations are forlornly confounded
Cherished expectations now look insubstantial and false

But the Father of Israel takes note
He will honour His covenant promises
He stretches out His mighty arm
He wields his sword of judgement
And confounds those who smugly boast
"God is finished with the Jews!"

The alliance of evil presses in
Inflicting an unspeakable suffering
Until, amidst great fire
It crumbles and falls, utterly destroyed (Judges 5:26-27)
Its members blown about like tumbleweed
By the furious rage of Yahweh
Their skin peeling off and their fat catching fire
Emitting a stench that will last for months

The killers of His people are no more
Their broken bones lie scattered across a burning landscape
Their charred remains smoulder
Acting as a spectacle and a warning to all of humanity
All of their schemes have come to nothing
Death has now become their final outcome
The end of their all-consuming hatred

NATIONAL DEGENERACY

The lamp of truth is smashed
All sense of decency has fled
A light of mercy fails to shine
The idea of purity has faded away

Morality has ceased to be
Self-control is now forsaken
The death of reason has taken place
Self-discipline is no more

Now a swarm of lies
Covers a filthy polluted land
Now an edifice of deceit
Rises from a deeply corrupted media

Those who once followed noble ideals
Look on, aghast and appalled
Those who once championed decent values
Now shake their heads in despair

Everyone seeks their own gain
No thought is given for tomorrow
Most of the population crave for nothing but pleasure
No consideration is given for the future

These are a people in love with folly
Decency has been replaced with carnality
These are a people who take delight in stupidity
Having regard for their own lusts above

The rich have become greedy dogs
Concerned with their investment portfolios
The pampered wealthy are consumed by lust
Always mindful of their luxurious properties

Behold, the worst excesses of Ancient Rome
Are now being repeated
Behold, the vile mysteries of Ancient Babylon
Are now being re-enacted

In stately homes Bacchalian orgies take place
Masked strangers groping with one another in the darkness
Mayfair Mansions open their doors to wild abandon
Silk-draped bedrooms echoing to loud orgasmic cries

Here is a nation abandoned to its folly
It languishes in thick black darkness
Here are a people given over to corruption
With pleasure the pinnacle of their desire

In city centres the young stagger and sway
Intoxicated with drink, crashing down on the pavement
In market town squares youths lurch and reel
Maddened by alcohol, they pick pointless fights

Girls vomit into the gutter
They defile their womanhood
Men urinate over war memorials
Mocking those who died for their liberty

Empty bottles and junk food cartons litter the pavements
A foul stench of vomit and urine pervades the night air
Smashed glasses and condoms strew the alleyways
Tension and violence fill the neon-lit streets

The protectors of children
Have become their worst corrupters
The guardians of little ones
Have defiled their tender innocence
By filling their minds with PC[10] confusion

What has Britain become?
What has happened to a once-great people?
What's gone wrong with our nation?
Why is there such depravity?

The United Kingdom has become a <u>dis</u>united Kingdom
Her leaders lacking any true vision
Great Britain has become an ungrateful nation
Her statesmen offering no solution to pressing problems

---

[10] In this context PC means *'politically correct'*

Political parties appease the extremes
Racist thugs are given media airtime
Men of violence are praised for their audacity
The murderer has become the hero

Spendthrift governments have ruined the economy
Creating an unsustainable Welfare State
The political elite have destroyed the Business Sector
Imposing bureaucratic burdens and destroying enterprise

The hardworking middle classes
Fear for their jobs and mortgages
Those aspiring to better themselves
Have had their fondest dreams dashed

Destitution has come to our once-rich nation
Pavement beggars now reach out everywhere
Poverty has replaced a precarious affluence
The homeless wander through empty shopping malls

Jobless people desperately look for non-existent work
They no longer have benefits to live on
The unemployed scan the media for vacancies
They no longer have any State Benefit

Mothers howl with maternal agony
They are unable to adequately feed their young
They sell, sell, sell everything (including their bodies)
To gain a meagre supply of food

Feral gangs fight to preserve their territory
Children torture and murder other children
Hordes of violent young savages
Cruelly torment the elderly and the disabled

Only the merciless wicked do well
Their many crimes going unrecorded
Only the scoffing evildoers thrive
Their vilest acts going unpunished

The *'thin blue line'* has broken
With many a policeman's beat long since abandoned

Steadily law enforcement agencies retreat
And each policeman's *'turf'* stands bereft and deserted

A famine of justice pervades the land
The weak go unprotected
Cynicism has replaced hope
The wicked go unpunished

Voluble news reporters babble into their microphones
Reporting a nation's descent into communal violence
Inside darkened bedrooms bloggers tap their keyboards
Describing the mayhem in their local neighbourhoods

Ranting, raving demagogues find an audience
As a simmering anger grips the masses
Loud, noisy hate-mongers begin to prosper
As a murderous disenchantment grips the young

A nation convulses in agony
But no one in the international community seems to care
A country breaks into pieces
But no one in the outside world is bothered

Britain no longer has influence
Its days of glory are gone
Britain is longer has credible
Its power has ceased

Abroad our armed forces are despised
They can't rescue our citizens
In foreign lands our army is in retreat
Terrorists mock our weakness

The people have departed from God
Everything has been ruined
The people have despised His Word
Everything is now desolate

A white dove has flown away
Leaving only strife and turmoil in its wake
A gentle presence has been withdrawn
With only hatred rushing in to fill the gap

A barbaric cruelty pervades the people
A land of gospel light
Now lies in utter darkness
Can anyone repair the lamp of truth?

PRINCE OF TERROR

How you have fallen, oh prince of terror
You who held the world in fear
Now you have become nothing
Your remains (like those of your victims)
Lie in an unmarked grave

Behold, Hell is astir at your arrival
The damned look up
And throw you a dead-eyed glare
Those whom you misled
Into becoming suicide bombers.
In their tormented bitterness they sneer
"Is this the paradise you promised us?"
Those whom you so casually murdered exclaim
"Hah! We've got justice at last!"
Former terrorist godfathers and tyrants from of old mock
"Where is your power and glory now?
Like us, you who were once so great
Have become nothing –
Why – you didn't even receive a state funeral!"

When relaying your death
Newsreaders barely concealed their smirks
There is widespread rejoicing
At how justice has been meted out
Only your fellow terrorists mourn
And, like you, they too
Will face an eternity of endless accusation
From those they misled

Welcome to Hell, oh prince of terror
It is your fitting home

THREE BROTHERS

In a far-off land there were once three brothers who'd inherited a vast estate from their kindly father. They'd received everything they could ever need, including land, animals and houses. One day the younger and middle brothers conspired against their eldest brother, saying *'Let's kill him and his family so we can increase our own fortune.'* This they did at night, leading a band of thugs to burn down his house and all who lived there, whilst they lay fast asleep. Later that night, as the two brothers were dividing up the elder brother's goods, the younger brother thought, *'My remaining brother is unmarried and childless. No one will care about him.'* So, the younger brother jumped on his remaining brother, slit his throat and threw his naked body onto the muck heap to be eaten by the dogs and birds. Pleased with his deeds the younger brother reclined on a luxurious couch, thinking *'My struggle has been successful. I'm now the most powerful landlord in the district. I fear no one and can use all of my brothers wealth to enjoy myself and expand my estate.'*

However, a few days later his neighbours held a secret meeting and decided *'Soon, he'll want to seize our estates too, so let's get together and slay him, along with his family. Let's gather a large band of armed men and attack his house on an especially dark night where there's not even a crescent moon shining.'* This they did, burning the younger brother's house down and all who dwelt in it whilst they were fast asleep. The next day the neighbours divided the estate, once owned by all of the three brothers.

Let those with ears listen carefully to the warning contained in this parable.[11]

---

[11] This parable concerns the relationship between Judaism, apostate forms of Christianity and Islam.

End Notes

Dates following the title show when each piece was first drafted.

A Judas Kiss: Saturday, 15th December 2018 – prompted by a reading of such Bible passages as Judges 2:25, Psalm 2, Matthew 24:13, Luke 18:8 and I Thessalonians 5:6-7, 2 Thessalonians 2:1-11 & 2 Timothy 2:1-9

Aquarian Era: 26th January 2009, but substantially modified on Thursday, 13th February 2020.

Beslan: Thursday, 9th September 2004 – when I was still in a state of shock about the Beslan High School massacre. It had taken place in Southern Russia on Friday, September 3rd 2004

Bigotry: Sunday, 1st February 2009; written to criticise all forms of bigotry

Bless You: January or February 1976 and rediscovered in November 2016

Bombed-Out Church: Friday, 10th October 2003. Sadly, the scenario portrayed in this meditation has become all too real in many areas of Africa, the Middle East and Asia

Entanglements: Friday, 10th September 2010 whilst practising Hebrew forms of poetry. It shows how the growing decadence within British Society is allowing *'the old evil'* of anti-Semitism to take root and spread

God Is Not Happy: Tuesday, 17th March 2009 after I'd heard (on television) a fourteen-year-old Pakistani boy claim he would volunteer to be a suicide bomber in order to *'make God happy.'* He was interviewed on *'Dispatches,'* Channel 4, Monday, 16th March 2009, broadcast 8.00-9.00PM

Old Horror: Friday, 10th September 2010, whilst trying to practice Hebrew forms of poetry. It explores the rise and then the final destruction of global anti-Semitism

National Degeneracy: Sunday, 13th September 2009

Prince of Terror: Tuesday, 3rd May 2011 (my fifty-fifth birthday) the day after the killing of the terrorist leader, Osama Bin Laden by American specialist troops. It followed a reading of Ezekiel 26:19f, 28:8-10 & 32:17f

Three Brothers: Wednesday, 21st January 2009

SCENE 2: THE FAITHLESS

1 Peter 4:17, *"For the time is come that judgment must begin at the house of God: and if it first begins with us, what shall the end be of them who do not obey the gospel of God?"*

ANGER

What is God's anger like?

It is like: -
A whirlwind, sweeping all before it
A tidal wave, swamping all before it
A blast-furnace, melting all before it
A sledgehammer, crushing all before it
And this anger is now
Breaking out against His Church

CHURCH OF SATAN

A Church of Satan
Is an adulterous harlot
A lover of perversity

A Church of Satan
Erects unaccountable hierarchies
Demanding unquestioned obedience

A Church of Satan
Possesses one set of standards for its leaders
And another for its followers

A Church of Satan
Secretly covers up its many abuses
Whilst quietly tolerating immoral behaviour

A Church of Satan
Concerns itself with its own survival
Rather than the wellbeing of its members

A Church of Satan
Thinks only of its own reputation
Choosing to ignore any injustice done to persecuted believers

A Church of Satan
Thinks only of its own status
Forever striving to widen its influence

A Church of Satan
Trusts in its own power and wealth
Rather than in the power and love of God

A Church of Satan
Binds its members up in unnecessary rules and regulations
Whilst condoning all manner of corruption in its leaders

A Church of Satan
Promotes docile conformists
Preferring unity in place of truth

A Church of Satan
Gives credence to every form of idolatry
And cruel forms of self-mortification

A Church of Satan
Buries biblical truth under the guise of *Tradition*
And vain scholastic speculation

A Church of Satan
Preaches many a false gospel –
Anything to hide the real work of Jesus

A Church of Satan
Dulls the truth behind a veil of mystery
Replacing it with a show of empty pomp and ceremony

A Church of Satan
Beguiles the masses with ritual
And many a bogus miracle

A Church of Satan
Deludes the unwary with silly superstitions
And spurious promises of blessing

A Church of Satan
Defrauds the poor of their hard-earned money
Whilst smoothly flattering the rich and powerful

A Church of Satan
Is a lover of wealth
And adores worldly power

A Church of Satan
Blindly conforms to worldly fashion
And is a willing slave to culture

A Church of Satan
Lacks any compassion
And is a stranger to mercy

A Church of Satan
Believes in its own infallibility
Spouting forth its unquestioned dictums

A Church of Satan
Is constantly ready to squash dissent
And persecute outsiders

A Church of Satan
Befriends many cruel tyrants
And pays homage to mass murderers

A Church of Satan
Cruelly exploits the weak
And endorses a range of dishonest practices

A Church of Satan
Is a true master of manipulation
And a lover of flamboyant display

A Church of Satan
Is willing to (openly or tacitly) support evil
In order to maintain its political power

A Church of Satan
Is cruel to women and children
Regarding both with contempt

A Church of Satan
May hide profanity
Under the guise of religion

A Church of Satan
Offers an easy way to perdition
And has ruined many a soul

A Church of Satan
May infiltrate slowly and unobtrusively
Into any and every Church assembly

A Church of Satan
May begin in <u>YOUR</u> congregation
Unless prompt discernment is exercised

HOUSE OF DARKNESS

The Church of God
Has become a house of darkness

Crammed with ambition
Headed for perdition
Full of lies
And many sighs
Lots of corruption
Plenty of destruction
Steely pride
Much to hide
Torrents of sorrow
But no tomorrow!

Weep for those whose hearts are bleeding
In prayer let us all continue pleading
Trust in the Lord
Don't be bored
Have faith in the Son
To Him let's all come

The Church of God has become a house of darkness
And what an awful sight it is!

HOW I GRIEVE

How I grieve for England's Christ-deserted Churches
How I mourn for its eternal loss
How I sorrow at its pointless degradation
Caused by decades of wilful apostasy

Church leaders and members have forsaken God's ways
They have betrayed His teaching and lost His blessings

In brooding sorrow, the Spirit departs from many Churches
Leaving them to useless man-made expedients

In a futile bid to stave off their further decline
They blindly follow the ways of a fallen world and the idols of this present Age

Oh, wretched Churches of England!
How blind you are!
How deceived and forsaken!
Wallowing in a darkness of your own making!

In justified outrage the God you've spurned will hand you over to the wicked

Those who hate you will become your rulers
Those who delight in heresy will *'lord it'* over you
Those who deride you will feel vindicated
And become smug in their contempt

The only future you now face is
Wrath – not blessing
Strife – not peace
Terror – not hope

In your selfish apathy you have betrayed the Lord
And shown disdain for His teaching
His Word you have spurned
Haughtily crediting it with little value

Nail-pierced hands are poised
To remove you from your lampstand
To cut off your witness to a corrupt nation
To shatter you into a thousand pieces

Truly, it is terrible to spurn the gospel of grace
To lightly abandon the only way of salvation
In your pride you have steadfastly refused
To accept that Jesus alone can give life
The voices of the prophets have all fallen silent
Now only a chilling silence remains

KEEP FAITHFUL

Keep faithful
Keep faithful to Jesus
And the teaching of scripture

Stand apart from the error
You are about to see
Rampaging throughout much of the Church

Keep separate from cheap sensationalism
Depart from those who make noisy claims
Whilst masking their iniquity
Under a guise of *'synthetic'* holiness
And empty platitudes

Weigh everything
Test everything
<u>Use your mind</u>
<u>Use your reason</u>
<u>Gather your common sense</u> –
Expose those ministries
Which do not come from Me

Oh, people of Christ –
Let His Spirit plead with you!
Stay firm in the faith
Do not follow the way of error
Yes, the High God

Who created the whole universe
By the words of His command
Implores you
To remember the sacrifice
Of His Son at Calvary!

Just as He was rejected by His own
Who *'knew Him not'*
So you too are about to reject Him
You give respectability to falsehoods
Which proceed from the pit

Will God have to come in judgement
Just as He did then?[12]
If so, it will be a terrible and mighty thing![13]

Let those who have ears
Listen and act upon the warning
His Spirit gives

Keep faith with Jesus
And in so doing
Avoid the seductive errors
Of the evil one

---

[12] A reference to the Romans' brutal crushing of the Jewish revolt and the subsequent destruction of the temple in AD70

[13] Perhaps the global financial crash (which began in September 2008) is the first phase of such a judgement. For many, it has truly been *'a terrible and mighty thing.'*

LEAVING

His Spirit has withdrawn

Leaving people to their own devices

Leaving people to die in their sins

Leaving people to the corruption of their own minds

Leaving people to pursue their own selfish desires

Leaving people to languish in their wilful perversity

Leaving people to follow the idols of their heart

Leaving people to indulge in long-cherished lusts

Leaving people to wallow in their own self-created filth

Leaving people to be swept away by bitter hatred

Leaving people to be moulded by a corrupt world

Leaving people to become shackled in spiritual darkness

Leaving people to be seduced by satanic delusion

Leaving people to be filled with demons

Leaving people to perish forever in the raging fires of Hell

SETTLING FOR DECLINE

Settling for decline
Settling for decline

There's no more that I can do
It looks as though we're through
You're settling for decline

I did my very best
But you failed to pass the test
You're settling for decline

Though allowed to have my say
You still chose the easy way
You're settling for decline

The announcement is so sad
Things could go so very bad
You're settling for decline

Once a Church of such distinction
Now you're heading for extinction
You're settling for decline

The old ways no longer work
My own duties I can't shirk
You're settling for decline

Our paths – which once converged
Are now separate and diverged
You're settling for decline

It's all become a bind
A fresh direction I must find
You're settling for decline

My energies are depleted
With separation now completed
You're settling for decline

My heart is set to break
This whole affair has made me shake
You're settling for decline

Things were given a real good try
Now it's time to say goodbye
'cos you're settling for decline …
Settling for decline
… An avoidable decline

STAND-UP

Stand up, stand up and be counted!
Choose this day whom you will serve
Would you serve His Son, the Lord Jesus Christ
Or would you turn to the empty philosophies of this world?

Stand up, stand up and be counted!
Choose this day whether to yield to Him
Or whether to continue going your own way
A way which will ultimately end in your total destruction

Stand up, stand up and be counted!
Choose this day by which Spirit you are filled
Or be seduced by that evil spirit which rules this world

Stand up, stand up and be counted!
Choose this day where your faith lies
In the Lord Jesus Christ and His sacrifice upon the cross
Or in your own empty strivings and futile thought-processes

Stand up, stand up and be counted!!
Choose this day who is to be your first love
The Lord God – Father, Son and Holy Spirit
Or some idol of your own devising

Stand up, stand up and be counted!
Choose this day all you who claim to be His people
Because He is drawing all of His faithful servants together
No matter what their denominational allegiance

Stand up, stand up and be counted!
Choose this day to make a life-changing decision
For, when it comes to dealing with God
You can't forever be pulling in two directions

Don't delay, for <u>now</u> is the time to make your choice

STONES

The *first* stone represents modernism
Which the Lord detests

The *second* stone represents superstition
Which the Lord abhors

The *third* stone represents corrupt bureaucracy
Which the Lord loathes

The *fourth* stone represents apathetic despair
Which the Lord will judge

The *fifth* stone represents bondage to tradition
Which the Lord will break

The *sixth* stone represents proud exclusivity
Which the Lord will humble

The *seventh* stone represents Jesus Christ Himself
Who will crush all of the other stones –
Grinding them into a thin powdery dust

THE WALL

After visiting the blacksmith's display at a certain agricultural show in the North of England, my family and I returned to the drystone walling area. There, a gang of skilled labourers were busily constructing a wall. Part of their technique included the *'chipping'* of certain stones into shape and the packaging of any spaces with small stones which had been left lying around. I also saw that various keystones (thrust right through the width of the wall) played a vital role in holding it together.

As I looked, the following allegory came to mind: -

God is building His Church
Like those labourers with that wall
Chipping people into shape
Fitting-in those
Who had once been alone and isolated

Look and see
God will raise up many keystones
Servants of the greatest *'Keystone'*
Jesus Christ Himself – God's only begotten Son

These will be men and women
Who will hold His people together
So that the work He has built up
For almost two thousand years <u>will stand</u>
And <u>not</u> crumble in the storms and floods
Coming upon this world

Look and understand
Be one of the keystones
Wait and you will see it happen
Say to Christ's true Church,
"You form part of God's wall –
A barrier against evil.
<u>*Stand firm, do not give in*</u>
<u>*To the pressure to compromise.*</u>
For that road leads
Only to endless destruction.

Provide a shelter
For people to enter and be healed
Remain true to Christ's teaching
Obey His commands
Rely upon the Holy Spirit's power
So that you will remain close to Jesus
Again, I say – AVOID COMPROMISE
And stay faithful to scripture."

TRUTH

He is the Lord
Who loves the truth

He is the Lord
Who guards the truth

He is the Lord
Who <u>is</u> the Truth

Yes, Jesus Christ is His name
And He is the Lord who expects the truth
From all who claim to follow Him

TURN

Turn
From your sin

Turn
To face reality

Turn
To Jesus Christ

Turn
To avoid Hell

Turn
To gain mercy

Turn
To obtain salvation

Turn
To know God
As your Father

Turn
And be filled
With the Spirit
So that you
Can walk steadfastly
Along the path
Of loving obedience

End Notes

Dates following the title show when each piece was first drafted.

Anger: Saturday, 25th October 1985. The last part was added on Sunday 21st October 1990 and slightly modified on Monday 16th March 2009

Church of Satan: Wednesday, 10th August 2011 whilst travelling on a Ferry from Douglas on the Isle of Man to Belfast in Northern Ireland, in extremely wet weather.

House of Darkness: Thursday, 17th October 2002; it theme expresses the darkness of the Christian Church in the Western World.

How I Grieve: Wednesday, 19th September 2012

Keep Faithful: Friday, 31st August 1990 as a response to the major heresy of the Kansas City Prophets (KCP) whose subsequent prophecy of a revival breaking out in England during October 1990 went unfulfilled. This resulted in much dismay within Charismatic and Pentecostal circles. The KCP debacle took place over a period of about six months prior to the October 1990 date. The struggle with this heresy proved one of the most difficult in my whole Christian life. In retrospect, it's clear that the Kansas City [false] *'Prophets'* were a mere prelude to the far greater deception of the Toronto Experience. Some of the ministries of these (so called) prophets were clouded by scandals involving alcoholism and immorality.

Leaving: Saturday, 11th September 2004; it's theme is the resulting devastation which follows the Holy Spirit's withdrawal of His protective grace.

Settling for Decline: Friday, 15th April 2011. During its composition I kept hearing the tune of the 1971 *'Doors'* Hit *'Riders on the Storm,'* which reflected my depressed mood at the time. A year later I had abandoned the Church in question – nothing else could be done.

Stand Up: Thursday, 22nd May 1986. There are definite times when God presents His people with a stark choice – to follow Him or to go their own way.

Stones: Tuesday, 3rd October 1989. First shared at a Christian Conference, it emphasises how God will judge the corruption within His Church. It had been preceded by a time of prayer in which I had *'seen'* a collection of stones lying in a dried-up-river bed which was also strewn about by weeds and other rubbish.

The Wall: Saturday, 16th May 1986; it emphasises how God wants His church to remain loyal to scripture. In the decades since this exhortation was written the pressures on Christians to compromise biblical standards has increased exponentially. Sadly, most churches have succumbed, preferring instead to offer a bland, watered down version of the Christian faith.

Truth: Tuesday, 19th September 1989. It emphasises the need to love the truth.

Turn: Sunday, 8th October 1989. It highlights the need for repentance in order to receive salvation. Performers may wish to repeat the word *'Turn'* three times.

ACT 2: THE CORRUPTION

SCENE 1: THE APOSTATES

2 Peter 3:3, *"Knowing this first, that there shall come in the last days scoffers, walking after their own lusts."*

BROKEN CHURCHES

One day in May 2006
As I strolled up a busy inner-city road
I saw two abandoned, boarded-up Churches
Two symbols of the death of faith
In what once had been *'Christian'* Britain

On my left stood a squat
Modern box-like building
Stained glass windows smashed
Daubed graffiti on the walls
I could see debris strewn across the floor of a vandalised hall
Where once, a congregation had sung praises
To a now neglected God.
Built in great zeal by voluntary donations
During the Charismatic boom of the 1960s
And under the leadership of elders
(Some from a solid Brethren background)
This congregation had, in their own way, fervently reached out
To their surrounding community
Preaching Gospel sermons
Promising that *'God was doing a new thing.'*
How vigorously they'd prayed for the removal
Of a succession of *'liberal'* vicars from across the road…
However, after years of faithful service
Each of the elders had retired,
Moving to be nearer their families
And, when enough money had been saved
Those left behind made a rushed decision to appoint a trendy Pastor
After all, the Church needed to look *'normal'* and *'respectable'*
Just like the others in the area

Their pastor zealously recommended (and then adopted)
The then latest charismatic fad which he labelled
'A lovely move of God from Toronto' –
A sudden phenomenon from a far-off land.
People had rolled about on the floor
Jerking like marionettes, controlled by a cruel puppet master.
Hysterical, cackling laughter
And animal noises had reverberated throughout the hall
(Whilst the crimson-painted words
'Holiness unto the Lord'
And *'We would see Jesus'*
Hung starkly from the rafters)
Women had fallen into orgasmic convulsions
As loudly proclaimed prophecies of a *'mighty revival'*
And *'Rivers of blessing in 1998'* were made, over and over again.
Grasping the sides of the lectern the slick performer would shout out:
'Let the fire fall!' or *'We want more Lord!'*
Or *'Come Holy Spirit, come <u>now</u> and bring revival!'*
…But revival did not come…

There came instead disillusionment, despair, division and defeat
The level of giving dropped
Money ran out
Debts were incurred
Bills went unpaid.
Dissenters – those unhappy with this *'move of God'*
Were accused of *'blaspheming the Spirit'*
Or of *'Blocking God's mighty work.'*
Finally, this same church was *'deconstructed,'*
(Whatever that meant)
Meeting only on an *'as need basis'*
The building was sold off
The proceeds helping this smooth-tongued Pastor
To purchase a new car
And to promote himself as a community-based interfaith *'peace activist'*
His smirking, well-groomed face
Appeared in the local newspaper
Amidst local councillors and other community leaders
His lack of Christian discernment
When in charge of this Church
Had left only catastrophic desolation
Now, in this modern box-like building nothing remained

Only a choking, dusty emptiness
All was dark and silent
As a once bright Gospel light
Had been snuffed out.

I looked across the road at a red-bricked
Late Gothic Revival
High Anglican Church
Also recently closed
Its windows boarded up
And, with narcotic-inspired graffiti
Daubed on its once pristine walls.
Its weed-strewn driveway
Led to a barred and weather-beaten panelled door
Now closed fast against the world
Surrounding this Church lay it's graveyard
Abandoned and completely overrun
With tangled briars and tattered bushes
Hypodermic syringes lay
Scattered amongst toppled headstones
And grandiose monuments, all tilted at crazy angles
Their once-proud inscriptions
Mockingly eroded by wind and rain
A cracked and mildewed notice board
(Announcing the times of High Mass
In faded, gilded lettering)
Now lay unheeded on the ground

This once respectable and *'oh so grand'* High Church
Had (pre-1914) consisted of Doctors, Professors, Solicitors
And wealthy, self-made businesspeople
Whose ears, each successive Sunday
Had been tickled by academic sermons
Extolling the new Liberal Theology
With its critical approach to God's Holy Word
And its accepting stance toward belief
In evolutionary human progress

But seventy years (and two World Wars) later
Things had changed
No longer the Doctors,
No longer the *'well to do,'*

And no longer the well-dressed ladies
Gossiping in the pews
They seemed but a dream
A thing of the past

By the mid-1980s
The congregation had fallen upon desperately hard times
And in all that remained
Were several arthritic, gossiping old ladies
And two elderly gentlemen
A chain-smoking caretaker
With a look of indifference
On his yellowing face
Would open the creaking doors
Exactly ten minutes after the service was due to begin.
A blond curate, sporting a dangling cruciform earring
Would enjoy mixing with tattooed working-class men
In a club he'd founded
But scandal had erupted
When he'd flung himself from the Church tower
His body splattered on the driveway below
It had been rumoured he'd just been diagnosed with Aids
Unpleasant allegations had ensued
And the club he'd founded was speedily closed
His vicar retired with a drink problem…
Or so another rumour had said
This man's successor had turned out to be
A raging fanatical priest in billowing black robes
Who'd strutted about on the cobbled side-streets
Amidst the worn, shabby red-bricked terraced houses,
Meanwhile, the local youths had looked on uncomprehendingly
Through narcotic-glazed eyes

Enthusiastic (yet totally undiscerning) for interfaith activities
This man would aim a quick, contemptuous sneer
At the *'pietistic sect'* from across the road,
Openly criticising them for wanting *'spiritual titillation'*
And all the while ingratiating himself
As an honoured guest at the local Hindu Temple
Newspaper cuttings showed him proudly officiating
At the first Gay Marriage Ceremony in the City -
Posing as a daringly radical priest

44

The Church authorities promoted him to higher things
And He became a Bishop in the South East of England

His successor was a lady,
A strange hippy-like creature
Who lived with a female organ player
(A larger, more nervous-looking lady)
After two years of celebrating the *'motherhood of God'*
In liturgies of her own devising
This lady vicar suffered a nervous breakdown
And both herself and the organ player had vanished to London
Or so it was said

What was left of the congregation entered nursing homes
Or quietly passed away
And so, the building had become impossible to maintain
And was duly closed
But no one would buy it

Now, two decades further on,
Its dripping, damp, cavernous emptiness
Reflects an inner spiritual emptiness
Which, in reality had always been there
This was a place in which the light of faith
Had <u>never</u> burned

Two broken churches
Each receiving a just recompense for their unfaithfulness
Each becoming a devils' den for vandals
And dead-eyed drug pushers
Each in their own separate ways had conformed to the world
And the world had utterly consumed them

BUSINESS AS USUAL

The congregation is ageing

Why bother to change?
Let's keep to *'business as usual'*

The membership is diminishing

Why bother to change?
Let's keep to *'business as usual'*

The Sunday school has closed because there's no children

Why bother to change?
Let's keep to *'business as usual'*

The *'Strategic Review'* recommends major modifications to our structure

Why bother to change?
Let's keep to *'business as usual'*

The changes proposed are designed to secure survival

Why bother to change?
Let's keep to *'business as usual'*

The leak in the roof will cost a great deal to repair

Why bother to change
Let's keep to *'business as usual'*

The stone cladding on the steps needs replacing

Why bother to change?
Let's keep to *'business as usual'*

The person who slipped on the steps is threatening to sue

Why bother to change?
Let's keep to *'business as usual'*

The blocked drains are creating an awful smell

Why bother to change?
Let's keep to *'business as usual'*

The financial situation cannot be sustained

Why bother to change?
Let's keep to *'business as usual'*

The community view us as being irrelevant

Why bother to change?
Let's keep to *'business as usual'*

The government is restricting religious freedom

Why bother to change?
Let's keep to *'business as usual'*

The law will force us to conduct same sex marriages

Why bother to change?
Let's keep to *'business as usual'*

Society around us is collapsing and our money is running out

Why bother to change?
Let's keep to *'business as usual'*

Transport has come to take us to the local Euthanasia Centre...

It's too late to change now!

COMPLICITY

What complicity!
What compromise!
What corruption!

Who can combat it?
Who can confront it?
Who can counter it?

Can anyone check the dire corruption
Engulfing both leaders and people alike
Within the Anglican Communion?[14]

Only those
Who have been strengthened
By God's Holy Spirit
And, from Him
Given a strategy to follow

---

[14] The two media sources cited in the Selective Bibliography confirmed that I'd seriously underestimated the extent of corruption within Anglican bodies like the Church of England. These sources explored the horrendous sexual abuses perpetuated by Bishop Peter Ball and the disgusting cover-ups that followed them. During these televised documentaries the Church of England came across as a cold and uncaring institution. The feelings of Bishop Ball's victims didn't seem to matter one tiny iota to its leadership.

COMPROMISE

A compromise here, a compromise there
It really is a total nightmare

Appease the enemy, appease the foe
What mighty troubles we hope <u>not</u> to sew

Be lovers of self, be lovers of power
Before God's Word we won't bother to cower

Chase after idols, chase after lies
There's no need for fear in <u>our</u> eyes

Devoted to sensation, devoted to healing
Crave for a cosy and warm *'high'* feeling

Doctrine is tedious, doctrine's a bore
'Blessed experiences' – we want more!

Fear not the Lord, fear not His Judgement
You know there's really no eternal punishment!

Follow a fashion, follow a trend
Let's all be the world's best friend

We hope in the Pastor, we hope in the Preacher
But we won't allow Jesus to be our teacher

Hunt after riches, hunt after wealth
Be absorbed in our own happiness and health

Let's have comfort, do as we please
Let's totally ignore our spiritual unease

Run after a craze, run after a fad
Laughing *'In the Spirit'* – let's go mad!

Surrender to this, surrender to that
No longer sulking under divine fiat![15]

---

[15] Here, the word *'fiat'* means divine rule.

Turn from truth, turn from God,
Stop being thought of as simply *'odd'*

Superficially happy and carefree are we
Our eternal fate we choose <u>not to see</u>

DEDICATED FOLLOWER
(Or how <u>not</u> to gain eternal life)

I am a most morally upright person
Who never succumbs to any form of vice
Or surrenders to any temptation

I'm a dedicated follower of the one true God
Oh yes, I am! Oh yes, I am![16]

No trace of corruption or any sin can be found in me
Perfection is a goal I've long since attained
All my deeds are pleasing to Him

I'm a dedicated follower of the one true God
Oh yes, I am! Oh yes, I am!

A lot of money I donate to charity
Many a good cause I graciously support
I even sit on wearisome committees!

I'm a dedicated follower of the one true God
Oh yes, I am! Oh yes, I am!

I despise those who aren't as good as me
I can't abide those who won't comply with my standards
I scorn all those who fall short of my ideals

I'm a dedicated follower of the one true God
Oh yes, I am! Oh yes, I am!

---

[16] At this point the audience may be encouraged to join in by responding *'Oh no, you're not! Oh no, you're not!'*

All sinners I view with utter disdain
Loose women I hold in particular contempt
Those not of my persuasion can go to Hell

I'm a dedicated follower of the one true God
Oh yes, I am! Oh yes, I am!

I regularly worship my dear sweet Lord
I painstakingly obey <u>all</u> of His commands
I gladly spend many hours in prayer

I'm a dedicated follower of the one true God
Oh yes, I am! Oh yes, I am!

I've never strayed in any single way
Even remaining faithful to a tiresome spouse
Many merits have I earned – all to please my Maker

I'm a dedicated follower of the one true God
Oh yes, I am! Oh yes, I am!

My conversation is all about holy things
Never a profane word falls from my lips
No *'naughty thought'* ever crosses <u>my</u> mind

I'm a dedicated follower of the one true God
Oh yes, I am! Oh yes, I am!

The quality of care I offer to others is excellent
The level of teaching I impart is simply profound
The type of leadership I provide is superb

I'm a dedicated follower of the one true God
Oh yes, I am! Oh yes, I am!

No fault or stain in my character can be found
I really am a nice saint to live with
A good and moral person is what I've become

I'm a dedicated follower of the one true God
Oh yes, I am! Oh yes, I am!

Complete humility I've already achieved
A *'holier than thou mannerism'* I keenly adopt
I am in truth, *'your ever so humble servant!'*[17]

I'm a dedicated follower of the one true God
Oh yes, I am! Oh yes, I am!

Many sweet experiences I can share
'Wonderful anointings' I have enjoyed
The power, the POWER is what I've received

I'm a dedicated follower of the one true God
Oh yes, I am! Oh yes, I am!

A fiery apocalypse I look forward to
The end of the world I gleefully anticipate
The damnation of all sinners I long to see

I'm a dedicated follower of the one true God
Oh yes, I am! Oh yes, I am!

Heaven's delights are what I've earned
(It's a pity about the rest of you)
Eternity with the Lord is my just reward

I'm a dedicated follower of the one true God
Oh yes, I am! Oh yes, I am!

On Judgement Day I'll remind Him of my virtues, saying
'Thank you Lord for not making me like other men' (Luke 18:11b)
'I'm sure you'll agree I've gained the right to enter your Kingdom'

After all ...

I'm a dedicated follower of the one true God
Oh yes, I am! Oh yes, I am! <u>Oh yes, I am!</u>

---

[17] A phrase used by the obsequious Uriah Heep in the Charles Dickens novel, David Copperfield

FAILURE

For over half a lifetime
I did my best – but to no avail
I worked hard – but saw no result
I tried my utmost – but for no reward
Things didn't come to anything
So why not completely abandon this frustrating God
And make a whole new beginning?

FOUNTAIN OF LIFE

Jesus is the fountain of life
Come, drink of Him
Oh you people
Abandon your dead works –
Deeds which arise
Solely from your own strivings –
Drink deeply of His Holy Spirit

In large bold draughts
Drink of Him
Gulp Him down with enthusiasm
Let Him give you the strength
To boldly witness to others
Jesus is the fountain of life
Come drink from Him
Oh, you people
Thirst for the Holy Spirit of God!

Let those who have ears
Understand that, should any church or individual
<u>Not</u> drink from <u>this fountain</u>
Then they shall surely perish through thirst
Or by drinking from a polluted fountain

HOW DID IT END LIKE THIS?

How did it end like this?

I do not know, but ...
It's all gone,
It's all finished,
It's all over

The rupture is now complete
Their smiling faces I will see no more
How did it end like this?
I just do not know

IN REALITY

They think they are free
But, in reality
They are the slaves of a cruel puppet master

They think they are above any law
But, in reality
They are being crushed by the *'law of sin and death'*

They think they are enlightened
But, in reality
They are becoming mentally darkened fools

They think they are knowledgeable
But, in reality
They are expressing the inanest stupidity

They think they are ascending into a higher realm
But, in reality
They are descending into the lowest regions of Hell

They think they are becoming divine
But, in reality
They are becoming worse than the beasts

Such is the fate of anyone who tries to be like God

LAMENT FOR A LOST FRIEND

You were the best of companions
One of the first to hear
Of my conversion in October 1975
And rejoice in the work that Christ
Had done in my life
How I enjoyed sharing my testimony with you
Until the early hours
You were a wonderful Christian
With a real concern for the poor
Your pastoral skills were superb
As was your ability to show compassion for the weak

In our youth we enjoyed
A sweet fellowship
Singing choruses of praise
And worshipping Christ together
Oh, how good and pleasant it was
To dwell together in unity (Psalm 133:1)

On a Holy Island Retreat
We watched a pale March sunset
Sink beneath a sparse Northumbrian Coastline
Enjoying a godly stillness
Broken only by the shrill cry of the birds

On monastic retreats
We would participate in the liturgy
Chanting our responses
And sharing the Eucharist

Late into a winter's night
We would discuss scripture
Probing its mysteries
And uncovering its teaching
On God's purposes for Israel.
We attended each other's marriages
And, as young parents raising children
Our fellowship continued
You displayed a wonderful hospitality
To my family

It was with delight
That I saw you grow into a mature minister
I could sense how you were loved
By those whom you cared for
You were one of the first
To see what I too could offer the Church

In a time of great personal crisis
You were of great help

Then …
For reasons that were a mystery to me
You became furtive
You failed to return my calls
And when I did get through
The answers you gave were evasive

A chilly coolness replaced our former warmth
With each of us harbouring a muted suspicion
In response, stern warnings were given but ignored
And the friendship between us died

Where did it all go wrong?
Why such cold evasion?
What caused the quiet antagonism between us?

Then years later
On a visit to Holy Island with my wife
I found an answer
A Church leaflet revealed that you were propagating
A false New Age spirituality
The idols of Eastern Mysticism had beguiled you
A training in Liberal Theology
Had besotted your mind
When its evil fruits should
At the very least, have exerted a healthy scepticism

As I'd once feared
God's Word was now no longer enough
Your excellent pastoral gifts
Were now engaged in misleading people

In the nicest possible way
Your once fine ideals now sadly perverted
To serve a useless nothingness

With dismay
I saw how you'd retreated
Into a *'Narnia Neverland'*
Where fantasy is mistaken for reality
And a toothless Aslan gives no roar

Now, you collaborate with worthless dreamers (Jude 8)
For whom Christianity is nothing but a fairy tale
They offer a healing which is not healing
And a therapy which is no therapy
You work happily with those
Who propagate pagan myths (Titus 1:14-15)
Seeing more *'truth in them'* than you do in scripture

'The spirit' you serve
Is no longer the Holy Spirit
But *'the spirit of anti-Christ'*
Who works assiduously to replace the truth with a lie

You have been handed over to deception
Yet to you, darkness is light
You have been handed over to folly
Yet to you, such folly is wisdom

You no longer discern where you are going
For the *'Prince of this World'* (John 16:11 & 1 John 2:11b)
Has distorted your vision
And darkened your mind
The light of the Gospel has gone out

Long ago you deafened yourself to all of my warnings
And error has been the result
For me this has produced a bitterly tragic vindication

Alas, I could weep for you
But inside I'm too numb for tears
Alas, I could bemoan and sigh for you
But inside I'm too stunned by grief

Alas, I could howl for the ruin of your soul
But inside I know that there'd be no point

The friendship between us is dead
The fellowship we once enjoyed is over
Restoration would take a miracle.
Because you have wilfully chosen to fully embrace this error
This second bereavement is worse than the first
Because I know we're now on different sides
In a spiritual war
We now have nothing in common

Why did you stray from the truth?
What foolishness possessed your mind?
Wasn't the high esteem in which others held you not enough?
Was your faith so weak that you had to resort to Buddhist meditation for comfort?
Didn't scripture provide the consolation you needed?
Evidently not
For you are friends with those
Who offer a demonised psychology

Oh, how I grieve for you, my ex friend
My former companion in Christ
For the chasm between us is unbridgeable
You have made a shipwreck of your faith (1 Timothy 1:19)
And there's nothing I can do

MONOCHROME

Black sombre bibles
Black hymnbook covers
Black knotted ties
Black two-piece suits
Black trilby hats
All reflecting a black outlook on life
They have turned the sanctuary of God
Into a funeral parlour
And then they wonder why
No outsider comes to their meetings!

MY LADY

Why did you fall my lady, my lady? Why did you fall?

What provoked you to desert your husband after decades of marriage?

Why did you fall my lady, my lady? Why did you fall?

What gnawing restlessness drove you
to take this reckless step?

Why did you fall my lady, my lady? Why did you fall?

What illicit passion made you seek comfort
in the arms of a stranger?

Why did you fall my lady, my lady? Why did you fall?

What good purpose can be served by the making of futile excuses?

Why did you fall my lady, my lady? Why did you fall?

What twisted perversity led you to flaunt your sin for all to see?

Why did you fall my lady, my lady? Why did you fall?

What future do you face after this cruel act of betrayal?

Why did you fall my lady, my lady? Why did you fall?

What marriage is safe after yours has come
to such a public and messy end?

Why did you fall my lady, my lady? Why did you fall?

What prevents others from viewing their own
marriage as *'just a friendship?'*

Why did you fall my lady, my lady? Why did you fall?

What will prevent others from following this downward
step of yours?

Why did you fall my lady, my lady? Why did you fall?

What encouragement have you given others
to copy your reckless action?

Why did you fall my lady, my lady? Why did you fall?

What more can be said about this wretched, squalid
affair?

Where are you going my lady, my lady? Where are you going?

Alas! We thought we knew you well
but, in reality, we didn't know you at all

Who were you my lady, my lady?, Who... WERE YOU?

ROLL-UP!
SEE THE GOSPEL CIRCUS SHOW!

Roll-up! Roll-up!
See the Gospel Circus show

Roll-up! Roll-up!
Get a nice cosy glow

Roll-up! Roll-up!
Hear a *'big name'* preacher tonight

Roll-up! Roll-up!
Be prepared for an astonishing sight

Roll-up! Roll-up!
We promise mighty miracles galore

Roll-up! Roll-up!
Allow your expectations to sore!

Roll-up! Roll-up!
Have no fear about the hype

Roll-up! Roll-up!
Enjoy preaching of a bold new type

Roll-up! Roll-up!
Bring your banker's card here

Roll-up! Roll-up!
Be delivered from all types of fear

Roll-up! Roll-up!
Listen to the rock band play

Roll-up! Roll-up!
Let the anointed preacher have his say

Roll-up! Roll-up!
Permit all inhibitions to go

Roll-up! Roll-up!
Enter a powerful new spiritual flow!

Roll-up! Roll-up!
Receive a wonderful new feeling

Roll-up! Roll-up!
Gain total inner healing

Roll-up! Roll-up!
Escape from every kind of bind

Roll-up! Roll-up!
There's no need to use your mind

Roll-up! Roll-up!
Generously fill our offering basket

Roll-up! Roll-up!
You don't want to leave in a casket

Roll-up! Roll-up!
If you wish to preserve your health

Roll-up! Roll-up!
If you hope to gain vast new wealth

Roll-up! Roll-up!
Drink of this brand-new wine

Roll-up! Roll-up!
Imbibe this blessing in double-quick time!

Roll-up! Roll-up!
Convulse on the floor if you'd like

Roll-up! Roll-up!
Laugh loudly through a mic

Roll-up! Roll-up!
Give the preacher all the glory

Roll-up! Roll-up!
Believe his each and every *'tall story'*

Roll-up! Roll-up!
This is happy-clappy party time!

Roll-up! Roll-up!
Everything's going to be just fine

Roll-up! Roll-up!
Loads of exciting drama

Roll-up! Roll-up!
Witness a grand panorama

Roll-up! Roll-up!
Much merchandise is on sale

Roll-up! Roll-up!
Expect to receive lots of free junk mail

Roll-up! Roll-up!
Click onto our widely used web site

Roll-up! Roll-up!
It certainly has lots of *'bite'*

Roll-up! Roll-up!
Please take your seats right now

Roll-up! Roll-up!
Wait for exclamations of *'ooh!'* and *'wow!'*

Roll-up! Roll-up
Make warfare against the foe

Roll-up! Roll-up!
Enjoy this cool <u>other</u> Gospel Circus Show!

SO MUCH

So much alienation
So much antagonism
So much anxiety

Surely this explains
Why I became estranged
From the Churches in this country?

So much delusion
So much disillusion
So much division

Does this not explain
Why I became depressed
By the Churches in this country?

So much failure
So much folly
So much futility

Does this not explain
Why I became so disillusioned
With the Churches in this country?

So much rejection
So much repression
So much resentment

Does this not explain
Why I decided to abandon
The Churches in this country?

So much pettiness
So much pointlessness
So much pride

Does this not explain
Why I now actively avoid
The Churches in this country?

So much sadness
So much sorrow
So much suspicion

Does this not explain
Why I no longer pray
For the Churches in this country?

For over forty long years I was on a *'road to nowhere'*[18]
It was a wilderness without end
But then, wholly unexpectedly
In April and May 2014
I began to find a refuge with an outcast people
God be praised
I was given a fresh start in my life
That allowed me to establish new friendships
That are precious to me!

---

[18] From the time of my confirmation into the Anglican Church (in November 1970) until my departure from the English Church scene, (around the Easter of 2012).

TAKING LEAVE
(A Poetical Reflection on the Death of English Christianity)

I <u>had</u> to leave the Churches in this country behind
There was no option – they'd become so blind

In the end, I couldn't take any more
Endless apostasy was all I saw

So many had become such a negative force
Their pointless ways unswervingly led to this divorce

They'd never wanted <u>anything</u> I readily provided
Spiritually, their hearts were completely divided

For many a fruitless year I sought to labour
And only rarely did my work find favour

The years I spent amongst them had been so very long
And now I ask myself – did I ever really belong?

Community responsibility they'd so casually forsaken
All the while refusing to consider they were mistaken

God's merciful grace was so constantly spurned
They incessantly viewed it as *'something to be earned'*

The world's vain baubles they wished to pursue
Blind to any consequences that would definitely ensue

Alas I saw so much delusion
The result could only ever be disillusion

My heart is filled with a deep well of sorrow
For most congregations there is no tomorrow

True doctrine many a Christian has forsaken
To perish in a wilderness of their very own making

The Churches in this country face a truly awful end
Having blindly followed each and every social trend

They continue to think that *'everything will be alright'*
Refusing to see they're no longer God's delight

For them Jesus is very far away
But this causes them no dismay

In fair England many Churches have died
Their wretched leaders having habitually lied

Pastors and Ministers can be ever so smooth
Offering an array of bland words to calm and to soothe

'People pleasers' was all they ever wished to be
No mention of hell – never wanting to see

Aiming for a good pension when they finally retire
Failing to see how stuck they are in a deep spiritual mire

Their aged congregations simply sleep and snore
They've ceased to wish for anything more

The roof has sprung yet another leak
But still the solid truth they refuse to seek

Financial resources are fast running down
And in the pulpit stands a garish clown

Most Churches are in a pitiful state
A cold and vacant apathy their most visible trait

Like the Church of Laodicea they've fallen fast asleep
In matters of faith they never went too deep

Death's cold fingers have begun to grasp them now
And soon they'll take a final arthritic bow

No modern-day revival ever truly came
Any huge gatherings were just a shadow of the same

Another Church closes – but who really cares?
Having once given itself such grand and *'respectable'* airs

English Christianity is now an arid wasteland
veering into a dense wall of sand

How Christ must weep over this tragic scene
And yet, from His eyes a holy rage must gleam

The house of God has fallen into ruin
A great deal of trouble is now seething and brewing

State persecution may soon be every Christian's fate
But, most won't see this until it's far, far too late

The Holy Spirit has now withdrawn
It's hard to believe in any *'new dawn'*

Only few bother to seek after God
Non-believers dismiss them as *'really odd!'*

I feel sickened at heart that most Churches barely stand
Great Britain is no longer a *'Christian land'*

Of a gathered remnant I see little trace
They appear to creep along at a snail-like pace

Some admittedly pray for revival
But most are preoccupied with daily survival

All this has been a very sore trial
As I pace up and down in brooding exile

There's no cause at all to celebrate
It's best instead to carefully deliberate

With English Churches it's now *'goodbye'*
They really aren't worth another try
Surely it's best to let them die

In my heart I still deeply mourn
My emotions have been so very torn
But in you, Lord Jesus, I've been re-born

THE PARABLE OF THE DRUNKARD

There was once a man who was going to be knighted by a King in a far-off country. Now this King was very stern and was known to expect the very highest standards from all of his subjects. The night before his honour the man stayed in a very luxurious five-star hotel, next to the King's palace. There he fell in with bad company; he got drunk and started to boast of his greatness. So drunk did he become that he vomited all over the place – even on the expensive suit he was to wear to the palace.

The next day he woke up with a dreadful hangover and was sick a few more times. Suddenly realising that he was late for the ceremony, he brushed his hair, cleaned his suit as best he could and rushed off to the palace. There he was stopped by a stern-looking guard who refused to give him entrance.
"Let me in, let me in" the man pleaded "I've got an appointment with the King. He wants to honour me, for I love him as a loyal subject."
To which comment the guard replied, "No one who really loves the King arrives late at the palace smelling of vomit."

The man was bound and thrown out onto the street where passers-by cruelly mocked him.

So it is with all those who willingly embrace deception.

YEAR AFTER YEAR

For year after year
I gave them my best
In teaching and preaching
Only to meet
With careless indifference
Cold rejection
Sullen apathy
And a complete disinterest
In all I had to offer

It's hardly surprising
That I now feel more at home
Amongst the outcasts!

End Notes

Dates following the title show when each piece was first drafted.

Broken Churches: Saturday, 7th October 2006. It expresses the desolation wreaked by apostate Churches. Each event is essentially true, with only minor details altered to preserve anonymity. Some of the incidents were combined from a number of sources. What remains is a regrettably accurate (if bleak) picture of the state of the Church in inner-city areas throughout the UK today. By July 2007, the first building (which had provided the model) had been demolished. A block of flats is now on its site. The other (red brick) building eventually became a cultural centre that does some good in the community. A graveyard from another closed church was included to heighten the impression of desolation.

Business as Usual: Thursday, 12th July 2012, approximately three months after I'd left the English Churches

Complicity: Monday, 26th May 2008. It expresses the dismay I felt concerning the level of corruption within the Anglican Church. It emerged whilst walking on a stony windswept path, inwardly praying whether I should tackle the manipulation being manifested at the 2008 Lambeth Conference of the Anglican Church. It was modified and updated on Thursday, 14th March 2019.

Compromise: Saturday, 25th June 1994. Written during a time when the deceptive Toronto Experience was breaking out across many churches in the UK. This particular satire is aimed at the attitudes found prevalent within many Western Churches at the time.

Dedicated Follower: Tuesday, 24th May 2011. It explores the way religious people may claim to be following God when in reality, the only *'god'* they follow is themselves. (The chorus was suggested by The Kinks' 1966 hit Song *'Dedicated Follower of Fashion.'*)

Failure: Friday, 20th January 2012. Written as my relationship with a particular Church was breaking down. We left there in April 2012.

Fountain of Life: Friday, 11th July 1986 – the final three lines being added on Friday 27th March 2009. It stresses the need to *'drink'* from Jesus in order to successfully live out the Christian life.

How Did It End Like This? Friday, 24th January 2013. I was overwhelmed by a crushing sense of personal inadequacy at the way things had gone with the English Churches

In Reality: Wednesday, 3rd March 2010, based upon earlier prose material.

Lament for a Lost Friend: Saturday, 21st August 2010, the day after a visit to Holy Island. It explores the emotional anguish experienced upon finding that a once-close Christian friend had embraced serious error. The *'first bereavement'* was the original loss of that friendship; the *'second'* the realization that this friendship could never be restored. This was because this *'lost friend'* had decided to propagate a deceptive and ultimately ruinous form of spirituality.

Monochrome: Sunday, 5th September 2010 – following a visit to a *'Strict and Particular Chapel'* with a small, ageing congregation. It exposes the depressing effect of dead forms of Christianity.

My Lady: Tuesday, 2nd November 2010 – after hearing that a mature Christian lady had claimed divine justification for divorcing her husband for another man. (She'd managed a highly regarded internet ministry which had blessed many people.) Later I'd seen a (long-since removed) YouTube video of this lady with this man in a hotel bedroom.

Roll-up: See the Gospel Circus Show: Saturday, 23rd November 1996. The main theme expressed here is the grotesque nature of a false, commercialised Gospel – one providing entertainment rather than showing people the way to God through Jesus Christ.

So Much: Wednesday, 31st May 2017

Taking Leave: Friday, 20th July 2012, approximately three months after I'd left the English Churches

The Drunken Knight: July 1998 after having confronted a Messianic Jewish leader for his involvement in the Toronto deception. This man was to subsequently reject the gospel – and a later view of his web site (on Monday, 4th May 2009) confirmed that he was promoting a mixture of *'cosmic awareness'* and a bizarre conspiracy theory.

Year after Year: Monday, 13th September 2013 – the last stanza being added on Monday, 30th June 2014 and amended on Thursday, 14th March 2019.

SCENE 2: MOTHER AND DAUGHTER

The Mother

Revelation 17:16, *"And upon her forehead was written a name, MYSTERY BABYLON THE GREAT, THE MOTHER OF HARLOTS AND ABOMINATIONS OF THE EARTH."*

ALAS

Alas, all Churches who replace
Truth with error
Right with wrong
Justice with injustice

Alas, all Churches who replace
Purity with impurity
Morality with immorality
Decency with indecency

Alas, all Churches who replace
Love with lust
Hope with despair
Faith with doubt

Alas, all Churches who replace
Order with disorder
Life with death
Clarity with confusion

Alas, for all such Churches
They possess
no integrity
no gospel
no future
Their demise is only a matter of time

BLOODY IRONY

In the dark confines of Callistus' Catacombs
I saw the tombs of third century popes
Magnificent in their day
Adorned with marble columns
And Greek (but not Latin) inscriptions
Here lay men of honour
Once tireless shepherds of a persecuted flock
Their beheading by the Roman Authorities
Had been a quick death
There'd assuredly been far worse ways
To have disposed of troublesome Christians!

Such was the fate of Pope Sixtus II
Betrayed and arrested when saying Mass
In honour of his martyred predecessors
Yet would he have celebrated that ritual at all
Had he known that his Papal successors
Would <u>also</u> kill and torture
Just as his Roman captors had done
To himself and his flock?

In the catacombs of Callistus
A terrible authority had begun to germinate
What had once been a Church of martyrs
Would later seek out its <u>own</u> martyrs
By fire and by sword
Slaying those it deemed as heretics
Leading to terrible divisions that continue even to this day
What irony! What BLOODY irony!

DEPART FROM ME
(The Fate Awaiting Many Popes on Judgement Day)

Surely Lord – there's been some mistake?
Did I not say many masses to merit your forgiveness?
Did I not offer many prayers to your Saints?
Did I not endlessly invoke your own mother, Mary herself?
Was I not zealous in persecuting heretics on your behalf?
How was I to know that some of them were yours?

(It was only a slip-up in administration; I was misled by my informants)

Lord! Lord! Lord!
Did I not commission exquisite works of art for your pleasure?
I employed the best artists you know – all at my own expense
Did I not authorise the building of many grand Basilicas in your honour?
Did I not erect proud monuments to glorify your Saints and Martyrs?
(Well at least <u>some</u> of them were your Saints and Martyrs)
Why – I even gave a portion of my wealth to the poor
I comforted them with indulgences to reduce their time in purgatory
And I even wore a hair shirt when I prayed for them
All this I did for your glory
(Not my own – no, no, of course not!)
Also, don't forget – I was a successor of Saint Peter
(It's a pity he's not here to put in a good word for me)

I'm sorry I mistook the goddess Astarte for your mother
Nor was it ever my intention to conflate you
With the pagan idol, Jupiter
Neither had I any wish to place more confidence
In the efficacy of dead Saints
Then in your blessed Holy Spirit

But, in humble humility
I must protest –
There <u>has</u> to have been some mistake!
I may deserve the odd year or two in purgatory
But surely no more!
If my own merits aren't quite sufficient to please you
Then surely those of the Saints and your own mother
Will have to do
Especially Saint Francis, for goodness sake!
What do you mean I failed to place my trust in your merits,
Or to believe that you offered the only complete sacrifice for my sin?
(Really, really – were my sins so very bad as to have needed your atonement anyway?)

Also, you state that I never once acknowledged
My need of you as my only mediator

But who are you to correct a Pope on such matters?
Can a true successor of Saint Peter be wrong –
As you say I am?
How <u>dare</u> you say that you *'never knew me?'*
Say that again and I may have to correct you –
Even excommunicate you!
No! I disagree! Mine was far more than just an outward form of righteousness
Comparing it to that of the Pharisees and Sadducees
Is utterly wrong and unforgivably defamatory!
Humph! If I was still in Rome
I would have you garrotted in the papal prison!
I would deprive you of the satisfaction of a public martyrdom!

Remember, <u>I</u> was your true representative
You must never forget that
Without me there would <u>be</u> no Gospel
After all, you needed a true and apostolic Church to preserve that Gospel!
On earth you depended upon me, Me, ME!
What do you mean?
Insinuating that mine was a *'false gospel?'*
I brought people into your sheepfold
Surely it is <u>you</u> who owes <u>me</u> a favour?
You can let me off a few centuries of purgatory at least

"What do you mean – there's no purgatory?"
How dare you order ME to depart into the everlasting flames?
Well, if that's your ungrateful attitude
I will leave you
You are now solemnly excommunicated
By my infallible decree
After all – I can propagate my own religion
Even in the fires of Hell!

DISAPPROVING GAZE

I scowl as I look steadfastly
Into his unseeing eyes
Before me is
A wooden statuette
Of Saint Dominic
Standing upon a pedestal
In a darkened side chapel –
Part of the dusty interior
Of Faro Cathedral in Portugal

A tonsured crown
Of curly black hair
Graces a cherubic
But lifeless face.
His arms are outstretched
As if making
A fervent appeal
His right hand holds aloft
A crude wooden cross.
His paintwork is faded
But he seems
To be wearing the robes
Of his Religious Order

There are many such chapels
Preserving the honour
Of this Saint whose zeal
For hunting heretics
Knew no bounds

I glare with baleful hostility
At this crude representation
Of a man who founded
An Order that soon became
The notorious Inquisition
Dominic himself
Was not averse
To supporting the odd massacre or two
In the Cathar territory of Southern France

If mistakes were made
And devout Catholics
Were slain – well, no matter!
God would know His own

Enveloped in an oppressive warmth
I reflected upon this shameless wooden effigy
'Your real memorial
Lies in the screams
Of those tortured in 'Inquisition Cellars'
Or burnt alive by the Order
You so zealously founded!
A church that honours you
Disgusts me.
Its leaders may as well
Have a representation of Himmler
Or Lavrentiy Beria[19]
Standing in your place.
On Judgment Day
Many who died horribly
At the hands of your Order
(And that of your crusading friend
Simon De Montfort)[20]
Will rise-up and accuse you both
What good then
Will all these chapels be
Erected in honour to your memory?'

---

[19] These were the heads of security who organized the torture and deaths of millions when serving under Hitler and Stalin.
[20] Simon de Montfort the Elder (c.1175-1218) was a French nobleman who led a bloody and murderous crusade against the Cathars in the period of 1209-1218. He died violently whilst besieging Toulouse. He was a friend of Dominic who would often stay at his headquarters.

HIDE IT

Hide it
Behind the priest
Behind the hierarchy
Behind the *'Holy Father'* himself

Hide it
Behind the saints
Behind the martyrs
Behind Our Lady herself

Hide it
Behind scholastic speculation
Behind volumes of Canon Law
Behind many Pontifical Decrees

Hide it
Behind glorious artwork
Behind white marble statues
Behind many beautiful treasures

Hide it
In the confessional
In many impressive ceremonies
In the celebration of endless Masses

'Hide what?' you may ask

Oh! I almost forgot –
The simple gospel message which proclaims that
As perfect God
Jesus Christ became perfect Man
In order to offer a perfect non-repeatable sacrifice
Which completely pacified God's justified wrath
Against all of our sins
He gives eternal life to those
Who believe in Him as their Saviour
And who trust in His merits alone –
And <u>not</u> in their own

Ah – then please understand –
If we dared to publicise that message
Then everything 'Mother Church'
Has so diligently built up
Over the course of centuries would simply crumble away
Our system would collapse, and chaos would follow
You see – we must remain silent and hide that most dangerous of messages
To preserve our institution and to maintain control
Over the souls of our dear people

LEERING SKULLS

The skulls grin
The skulls leer
The skulls smirk
At the inquisitive tourists
Visiting Faro Ossuary

Jammed between
Leg bones
And neatly arranged
In soaring columns
They cross over
A rounded ceiling
Gazing with
Sightless mockery
At the floor below

Most of them were friars
Eking out lives
Of fasting and prayer
Broken only by
The occasional visit
To an odd brothel-or-two
Or forced intimacy
With a younger brother
Some may have watched
The last auto-de-fé –
'Acts of faith'
Where the screams

Of burning heretics
Would have been
A sweet melody
In their ears

To their way of thinking
The infallible authority
Of Holy Mother Church
Will have been vindicated!
After all, wouldn't their killing
Restore God's natural order
And prevent earthquakes?
Persecution was surely the means
To earn the favour of Jesus Christ!
Without doubt, He would honour
The firm stance taken
Against such devilish error

But now their life stories
Are an inquisitorial secret
No confession of sin
Comes from their ebony lips
Their loves, their lusts
Their devotion, their debaucheries
All forgotten

Instead …
There remains only
The silence of the dead

LOATHING
(Written from the Viewpoint of an Old testament Prophet)

How the Lord must loathe
Your gaudy ceremonies and masses
How He must detest
The way you suppress His Gospel
Behind a pagan pantheon of superstition
Portrayed by your images and statues of Astarte![21]

He hates your hierarchy of fear
With its many cruel deceptions
He despises how you look to earthly powers
And not to His precious only Son, Jesus Christ
The Word made Flesh
The way you venerate dead *'saints'*
Adorning their skeletal remains with jewellery and medals
Is an abomination that sickens the Holy Spirit
You show more interest in them
Then in the living Christ Himself!
Is it not a vain and futile thing
To look for life and blessing
Among the dead?

The endless adulteries you commit are tedious
Your hope is to favourably influence the Lord
By praying to His mother Mary and the Saints

You remain wilfully blind to the fact that
*"There is only one mediator between God and Man –
The man Christ Jesus,"* (1 Timothy 2:15)
The way you idolise other *'mediators'*
Wholly betrays your total lack of trust in Him

How you allowed and *'Covered up'*
The systematic abuse of children
Makes the Lord want to vomit you up
The hypocrisies of your hierarchy are endless
As your punishment will be in the fires of Hell

---

[21] A pagan goddess of war and sexual love in the Ancient World.

Has not the Lord
Creator of the Heavens and the Earth
Heard the sobs of countless children
Raped by your priests?
Has He not counted every tear
That has fallen from their faces?
For the sake of those little ones
His wrath has been kindled
He will deal with abusers
And those who protect them
In the fulness of His anger
The hammer blows of judgement <u>will</u> strike!

Yet, you vainly boast of your power and influence
You babble on about your great artwork in the Vatican
Not realizing that Michelangelo's painting
Of *'The Last Judgement'*
Was a divine commission –
Designed to warn all hierarchies (including yours)
Of their eternal fate unless they repented
The Lord chose to speak in this distinctively visual way
To enable you to understand
Those things which may await you on Judgement Day
For was not the Lord's Spirit with Michelangelo
As He had been with the craftsman Bezalel
During the construction of the Tabernacle?

Yet, by God's grace
There remains a remnant amongst you
Who are God's Children
Who show compassion for the poor
And who care for the homeless
Who bravely oppose moral and political corruption
Whose true good works are greater
Then when they first began
Most assuredly, there will come a time
When God will bring judgement upon your *'system'*
It will be handed over
To the one who will usher in a global deception
Resulting in horrendous destruction upon the whole world
Your institutional pride will come crashing down
And be brought to absolutely nothing

PRISSY PRIEST

In Vatican Square
Whilst standing next to a gushing fountain
And *'tourist trap'* Ticket Office
I saw a prissy priest walking by
He wore a black cassock
A black floppy hat
And narrow black rimmed glasses
A look of constipated strain
Creasing across his face

Whoosh! Into his body I went – to record his thoughts
And to take note of his prejudices

"I am a humble priest
Of the one true, Holy Catholic and Apostolic Church
I offer up the body and blood
Of Jesus Christ 'Ex opere operato,' [22]
In my devotion to Mother Church
I propagate true Catholic doctrine
I honour the Saints and especially Our Lady
I would never deviate one word
From what the 'Holy Father' teaches
To me his word is law
To be unquestionably obeyed
With no further thought or dissent

Furthermore, I hate all of the heathen
I despise every disgusting Sodomite
And all other foul perverts too
I value the gift of poverty
I've even given up the prospect of Holy Matrimony
To become a faithful son of the Church
How pleasing I must be to you, oh Lord!
How holy must I be in your sight!
How you must delight in all of <u>my</u> good works!

---

[22] This is a Latin term meaning *"from the work worked"* It refers to the belief that the sacraments are efficacious (effective channels of divine blessing) in and of themselves. Their use is <u>not</u> dependent upon the attitude (or behaviour) of either the minister or the recipient.

Truly, I am not like other men
And certainly not like these scantily clad tourists around here!
Disgusting! The women especially!

In contrast
I serve the poor
I hear many a confession
I do my very best to be a good priest
And I try to love those whom I find most difficult
Even that Father Rackety who does so love his whisky!

By my own efforts I will acquire the merits to enter Heaven
(Or at least to vastly reduce the number of years I spend in Purgatory)
I will achieve righteousness
Through the good offices of our Lady
To whom I pray every day, without fail
Yes, I am a devoted son of the Church
Fervently obedient to every single one of its teachings"

Whoosh! I exit his body
My work of recording done

Angrily, I look at him and think
"Fool! Don't you realize
That all of your righteousness is as filthy rags? (Isaiah 64:6)
One day conservative priests like yourself
Will be tossed aside
When The Vatican finds it politically expedient
To change its policy
On homosexuality and same-sex marriages
Also, will you still be thinking 'holier than thou' thoughts
On the day terrorists storm
Your small mission church in Africa
And your soul is required by God?"

PROUD ROME

Oh proud Roman Catholicism –
How much you are in love with yourself!
How, under a veneer of false humility
You love to display
Your beautiful art works
Your wonderful treasures
And your relics of dead Saints!

In private, your officials
Boast about their influence in the world
Adopting a false *'bonhomie'* – even with their Mafia contacts
After all – can't such sins simply be *'confessed away?'*
And there's always the good offices
Of *'Our Lady'* to rely upon
She will successfully mediate between the sinner and God

Yes, in worldly terms you have almost everything
But in reality you have nothing
For you are without the simple Gospel of Jesus Christ
Which most assuredly proclaims
That Jesus Christ was the Word made flesh
Who came into the world to save sinners
And <u>to abolish the need for any priestly hierarchy</u>
Or for any other sacrifice

Oh, proud Roman Catholicism –
How much you glory in your traditions!
But one day your finest achievements
Will be as dust
For this world – with all of its vain pomp and glory
Will simply pass away (1 John 2:15-17)

SHAKING OFF

This was the rubbish that our esteemed and holy fathers deemed useful to fill our minds: -
- A hatred of the Jews and Judaism itself
- Fear of a priesthood – whose authority was to be accepted without question
- Contempt for women – viewed as the seductive *'daughters of Eve'*
- Dependence upon Icons and other idolatrous objects
- Subservience to unjust political authorities
- A slavish devotion to Mary and the Saints
- Vain hope in a man-made system of gaining merit with God
- Cringing reverence for Bishops, Patriarchs and Popes
- Terror of a non-existent purgatory
- Respect for an *'Institution'* that destroys the innocence of children
- Contempt for all those with Same-Sex Attraction
- The expectation of silence and secrecy from the victims of abuse (after all, disclosure would undoubtedly bring dishonour and disgrace to *'Mother Church'* and the possibility of eternal damnation)

In the name of Christ
Let us *'shake off'* these many lies
Let us return to the *'One True Faith'*
As revealed in the inspired Word of God
And the simple Gospel of Jesus Christ –
Wherein NONE of the above apply!

TOUCHING THE FOOT

From all nations and backgrounds they come
By land, sea and air they come
In a spirit of fervent devotion and craven superstition
They come to touch the foot of Saint Peter's statue
Then, bowing to a statue of Mary (or some other graven image) they say their prayers
Whilst desperately hoping that a long dead saint
Would intercede on their behalf
All are very pious
All are very religious
All are very reverent
But alas, these are a people
Betrayed by a Church
That prefers to entomb the truth
That Christ is the only mediator
Between ourselves and God
And that, out of love, He died to save us from these very same superstitions
Which are simply the Vatican's playthings

End Notes

Dates following the title show when each piece was first drafted.

Bloody Irony: Saturday, 31st August 2013. Written in a Youth Hostel bedroom and inspired by a visit made to the Catacombs of Callistus on Tuesday, 20th August 2013

Depart from Me: Sunday, 8th September 2013

Disapproving Gaze: Thursday, 4th October 2018. Written when reflecting upon an earlier visit made to Faro Cathedral on Tuesday, 21st August 2018

Hide It: Saturday 30th August 2013. Written in a Youth Hostel bedroom, inspired by a visit to a variety of Catholic sites whilst on holiday in Rome. (Our holiday lasted from Saturday 17th to Friday 23rd August 2013).

Leering Skulls: Thursday, 4th October 2018. Written whilst reflecting upon a visit paid to Faro Ossuary on Wednesday, 22nd August 2018

Loathing: Sunday, 8th September 2013. It examines what an Old Testament Prophet would most likely say about today's Roman Catholic Church.

Prissy Priest: Friday, 30th August 2013. Written in a Youth Hostel bedroom. It was initially inspired by seeing a Catholic Priest in the Vatican on Monday, 19th August 2013. My immediate thought had been, *'What must be going through the head of such an unhappy-looking man?'* His facial expression had suggested (to me) that he was trying to persuade himself that he was right with God when deep down he knew he wasn't.

Proud Rome: Tuesday, 10th September 2013.

Shaking Off: Saturday, 20th July 2013

Touching the Foot: Tuesday, 10th September 2013. I'd concluded that Roman Catholicism will happily integrate with any religious influence as long as it's not the simple Gospel of Jesus Christ. As an Institution, its far more *'Cosa Nosa'* (Mafia) than *'Paternoster'* (Our Father)!

A reading of Martel's (2019) excellent and well-researched book, *'In the Closet of the Vatican'* would suggest that all these pieces had seriously underestimated the corruption pervading senior levels in the Roman Catholic Church. Clearly, it's a body that has forfeited any true spiritual authority it may once have possessed.

The Daughter

Revelation 3:16, *"So then, because you are lukewarm and neither cold nor hot, I will spew you out of my mouth!"*

ANGLICAN ANARCHY[23]

Oh, you Saints in Heaven and on Earth
LISTEN AND HEAR
Tremble at the Lord's awesome acts
Quake at the display of His Holiness
For He has borne His mighty arm of war
Against a corrupt, rebellious, polluted hierarchy
And He will STRIKE them in His holy anger.
Listen, pay attention and concentrate
On what is going to be shared.

Through the anarchy of Anglicanism
God is confronting
Complacent evildoers and rebels
Whilst separating
The faith<u>ful</u> from the faith<u>less</u>

Through the anarchy of Anglicanism
God is confounding sneering skeptics
Whilst strengthening harassed hearts
And fulfilling the promises of His unerring Word

Through the anarchy of Anglicanism
God is doing a great work
His Gospel WILL be witnessed
His Spirit WILL erupt with power
His Truth WILL be proclaimed
Whilst forgiveness WILL be granted
To those who believe in His Son

So be comforted, GO and praise His Holy Name.

---

[23] The word *'anarchy'* refers to the chaotic lawlessness that results from a collapse in government authority.

BISHOP OF SIN

I was the Bishop of sin
My own praises I loved to hymn (la-la-la!)
The old prayer book I flung in the bin
A close friend of Rowan was I
But now that's all bye-the-bye

At Eton I was educated
From Oxbridge I graduated
Liberal Theology was what college taught me
It wrecked my faith and I'm now *'I'm all at sea'*
Discovering that Scripture was only a story
And that Creeds were old fashioned and hoary
It destroyed what little belief I once had
And for a while, I felt bereft and sad

As a curate I once did serve
The vicar said I had a nerve
To hang my doubts out on display
With angry parishioners showing great dismay
The Eucharist I was there to celebrate
But still the vicar I would infuriate
In a theological cemetery (oops seminary)
I went to teach
The one true Gospel was something
I couldn't preach
But still I was a very good *'wordsmith'*
Showing how scripture was all a myth.
Theological reports I summarised
Choirboys I sodomised
My fervent passion
Lay utterly with doctrinal fashion

Promotion came my way
The *'old boy'* network I could play
The right boots I learnt to lick
In Church politics I practised every trick
In a large Cathedral I went to work
Not even the smallest duty did I shirk!
A veneer of spirituality I soon acquired
An attribute that most certainly was required

In soft light tones I learned to speak
No matter if to some I looked a freak
Gregorian chants I used to sing –
But they were never really my thing
Angry Canons I would soothe
In that Cathedral I was ever so smooth
In gaudy robes I loved to flounce
On cherub choirboys I would pounce
I thought *'Those like me will have our day*
No matter what 'Reactionary Traditionalists may say'
To scotch wild rumour I got wed
But *'phew,'* no children were ever bred
My wife would endlessly complain
For everything I'd get the blame

Separate lives we agreed to lead
On this our hearts were not to bleed
She amused me with her chatter
About things that didn't really matter
My late mother she did resemble
Oooh! That face I could disassemble
Now a dear old thing
With that large wedding ring
A reminder of our nuptial vow
To which I wholly refused to bow.

Cannabis I decided to smoke
Whilst treating it lightly as a joke
Very radical I wanted to seem
Although to some a trifle *'off-beam'*
Media attention I craved to gain
A public reputation I wished to claim

Church unity was my favourite game
And on this issue I would not be tame
In the dear Pope I placed my hope
(Must have smoked too much dope)
Those rigid Evangelicals I loved to annoy
By treating scriptural truth as a toy
Other faiths I gently wooed
My critics I certainly quickly sued
On important committees I sat

90

Doing *'a lot of this and a lot of that'*

My own Bishop I learnt to flatter
With a great deal of honeyed patter
Got a name for getting things done
Even though I was a meddling fool to some.
Promotion was what I sought
Heresy was what I taught.
Durham, Oxford or York I would accept
My career in stone was set
Not for me the see of Canterbury
For that attracts too much publicity

At last I got promoted
As a rival was demoted
The Bishop of sin I became
Things could not remain the same
I employed every legal ploy
Against those lives I wished to destroy
The threat of a writ made a big hit
And landed my enemies in a pit
In the occult I learnt to dabble
(When of course not playing scrabble)
'Good and evil are one'
That argument has assuredly been won
Visions and dreams I received
My critics said I was deceived
In my eyes I became like a god
To me that wasn't all that odd
In my pride I had only my own sins to hide
Especially from her who had been my bride.

Memoirs I wrote when I retired
Requiring lawyers to be hired
I'm afraid sales didn't exactly soar
And reviews were upsettingly rather poor
A soul greatly missed was I
When once I breathed my last sigh
Many were the (hopefully heartfelt) praises
Of my life in all of its varied stages
Eulogies were read aloud
My many virtues would make anyone proud

Soft music was heard to play -
I wish I could have had my say.
My body was consigned to the ground
As my widow made a loud weeping sound
She certainly managed to put on a good show
And a splendid wake she absolutely did throw!
However, I saw her secret look of relief
Now, that really was beyond belief
Alas, my grave with weeds is overgrown
As I fully see what my life has sown
No one bothers to visit it now
I'm quite forgotten, I don't know how!

I was once the fashionable Bishop of sin
But my own praises I can no longer hymn
Because in Hell there's an overwhelmingly, frightful din

HOW DARE THEY?

How dare they welcome
Persecuting evildoers into the Assembly!

How dare they share
The body and blood of God's Son
With those who hate His followers!

How dare they misuse
His Eucharist to give credibility to heretics
Who flout God's Word!

Great indeed is their guilt before heaven
Miserable will be their fate
Wretched is their destiny

In their arrogance
They believe they are *'above all accountability'*

In their complacency
They hope to impress the world
With all of their empty ceremonies
In their pride

They think God will do nothing

To them, sharing the Lord's Supper
With those who follow false gods is acceptable,
'Erroneous and strange doctrine, contrary to God's Word'
Is welcomed
'The peace' is shared with those
Who teach and live a lie
Bringing hurt to God's people

They do not see
Because
They do not wish to see

They do not hear
Because
They do not wish to hear

They do not understand
Because
They do not wish to understand

Their ways are dark
And their minds befogged in a comatose stupor

In broad daylight
Will their disgrace be seen!

In fading twilight
Will they stumble and fall!

In pitch black darkness
Will they be given over to confusion!

From heaven the Holy One of Israel
Sees how they exploit the sacred elements
To chase after an imaginary unity
That makes light of the abuse
Suffered by adults and children alike

In His outrage God <u>will</u> act
Confounding those who

Would use His Eucharist
For their own ends
Consuming the bread and the wine
Without due discernment

Do not babble
'We have tradition, tradition, tradition!'
For if you had
You would not have given respectability
To those misusing secular courts
To fret and harry God's people.

Alas for those Traditionalists
Using Holy Communion
As a respectable *'cover'* to accommodate evil
They have disgraced themselves before God and Man
In their eyes a feigned *'group solidarity'*
Is more important than the common-sense values
Of decency, honesty and truthfulness

Alas too for a Church having *'slipped its moorings'*
Aimlessly floating like a rudderless oil tanker
About to crash onto needle sharp rocks
Great is the pollution
That will ensue.

HOW MANY?

How many routes
Must you consider?

How many avenues
Must you enter?

How many paths
Must you explore?

How many roads
Must you travel?

How many detours
Must you follow?

How many dead-ends
Must you encounter –
Before you're willing
To walk with
Jesus, your Lord?

NEW AGE WOMAN

There you sit, hunched over your tarot cards
Having already consulted your spectral spiritual guides
You keenly advocate alternative health therapies
With crystal healing as your latest *'fad'*
A turquoise necklace gracefully hangs
Atop your long loose dress of a 70's hippy design
Copper bangles adorn each of your wrists
And your short bobbed, jet black hair
Frames a plump *'earth-mother'* face
Major decisions you refuse to take
Unless Mercury is aligned with Venus
And each star is residing
In its most auspicious heavenly sphere

Counselling is your main vocation (wherein you most excel)
You welcome many a distressed female client

Into your Feng Shui-oriented *'surgery'* [24]
Surrounded by soft, calming music.
African masks adorn the walls
And small goddess statuettes line the mantelpiece
Hinduism, Buddhism, Sikhism
Judaism, Christianity, Islam and Atheism
All are the same to you
But deep inside you still long for *'The Maitreya'* –
The great World Teacher who will embody
'The Christ Principle' and rule the whole world in love
He will usher in a new Aquarian Age
Of harmonious enlightenment
Ah – such a welcome future

With measured deliberation you sup your herbal tea
From a daintily patterned china teacup
Quietly scanning your lecture notes
On *'Finding the goddess within'*
You purr with satisfaction
Over how you will help to bolster
The fragile self-esteem of those women
Scheduled to attend this evening's Theosophical meeting
Where you will consult with the spirit of its founder
Madam Helena Blavatsky

Life is good,
You are happy and you are fulfilled
After all …
You are the Pansexual, Buddhist, Radical Feminist
Reverend Philippa De Foxley
(Better known as *'Pippa'* to your friends)
Partner in a three-way marriage relationship
(Don't ask, it's complicated – one's an android)
Ordained priest in the Anglican branch
Of The Global Ecumenical Church
Popular author of spiritual *'self-help'* books
Television celebrity, social media sensation
And Bishop in waiting

---

[24] Pronounced *'Shu'* or *'shoe.'* It's a Chinese mystical practice, involving aligning furniture and fittings in such a way as to channel a flow of positive energy and create an atmosphere of harmony.

RITUAL DEFILEMENT

Woe to a Church with leaders
Who know no boundaries

The world scoffs
The brethren are scandalised
Angels turn away and blush
At the demonic defilement
Of Christ's sacred ritual

Woe to a Church with leaders
Who provoke God's wrath

What hope is there now for Anglicanism?
What hope is there now for its proud prelates?
What hope is there now for its sleeping congregations
Who pretend that everything is alright
And that all will go on as before?

Woe to a Church with leaders
Who stumble in a darkness of their own making

How long, oh Lord, will you allow your grace to be abused?
How long, oh Lord, will you allow your mercy to be mocked?
Will even you, in all your love, allow your sacred rite
To be manipulated to serve a corrupt political agenda?

Woe to a Church with leaders
Who are beyond repentance

See how these blasphemers drink deeply
From your cup of wrath!
Observe how supposed representatives of your Son
Make a mockery of His Holy Name
Perceive how things go from bad to worse
With corruption spreading like a devouring cancer
From top-to-bottom

Woe to a Church whose leaders
Treat Holy Communion as a political toy
Striving to promote a unity that <u>doesn't</u> exist!

Can there be any hope of healing?
Can there be any hope of restoration?
Can even you, oh Lord cure the idolatry
Created by those who've rejected your Word?

Woe to a Church with leaders
Who are under severe judgement –
Mass delusion will follow their ministry

SMALL AMBITIONS

My aim?
A comfortable living

My objective?
Social acceptability

My ambition?
A respectable position
Conferring a certain status in the local community

My desire?
To get along with people
And to be highly regarded

My stance?
One of inclusivity
And openness to contemporary cultural trends

My approach?
To *'affirm'* everything my <u>dear</u> people want
I really am reluctant to say *'no'* to anything

My means?
To smile and nod and agree with everything they say
(I avoid *'making waves'* as there <u>is</u> my pension to consider)

Oh, my name?
It's the Reverend Small-Beer –
Here's my card

THE ANSWER

Why is the Church in such a mess?

The answer is proud unbelief[25]

Why do so many Christians wallow in sin?

The answer is proud unbelief

Why are God's gifts so cruelly mocked?

The answer is proud unbelief

Why is God's Spirit so completely absent?

The answer is proud unbelief

Why is false teaching so readily accepted?

The answer is proud unbelief

Why is Christ's Gospel so completely ignored?

The answer is proud unbelief

Why is heartfelt preaching so often futile?

The answer is proud unbelief

Why do so many Christian marriages end in divorce?

The answer is proud unbelief

Why are so many congregations torn apart by internal strife?

The answer is proud unbelief

---

[25] Performers reciting this piece may repeat the refrain *'The answer is proud unbelief'* to further emphasise this point.

Why are many denominations so corrupt?

The answer is proud unbelief

Why do Church organizations forget their mission?

The answer is proud unbelief

Why is much worship so tedious?

The answer is proud unbelief

Why doesn't God answer our prayers anymore?

The answer is proud unbelief

Why has the love of many grown icy cold?

The answer is proud unbelief

Why will many churchgoers end up in Hell?

The answer is proud unbelief

THE STROKE OF A PEN

It was a simple thing –
Penning your signature to a Report
One that would stumble
Little ones in Primary Schools
The stroke of a pen did it –
It was a bureaucratic chore
Nothing more!

Some positive media coverage was created
A much-needed favourable image generated
And public embarrassment, thankfully, avoided

Dissenters in your Communion
Were safely ignored
What do their Conferences (run by *'Ginger Groups'*)
In faraway places matter to you?
They were nothing but a mild annoyance
A wearisome irritant to your authority

But through that one signature
You risked generating a whole cascade of abuse
That will assuredly shame you for all of eternity

What's this I hear?

A desolate crying, howling, sobbing and moaning

What is it
But the handwringing anguish
Of decent Christian parents
Their little ones
Having been snatched by
By the *'politically correct thought police'*

Their crime?

To teach that God created only men and women
And not a plurality of genders
A complaint was made
'Diversity Enforcement Officials' were called in

Matters were passed on to the police
And a *'Care Order'* issued
Two more youngsters
Were sent to an already crammed
'Children's Rehabilitation Centre'
'Taken into care for their own welfare
Parents guilty of hate speech
Charges have been made'

Another *'State-based kidnapping'*
Has taken place – but none of the Bishops care
'After all, they were only Fundamentalists
And really, it was all for the best.'

Alas for the *'nodding donkeys'* of political correctness
Within the Church of England
Who prefer to retain
A distant *'diplomatic'* silence
Despite the suffering
Inflicted on parents and children alike
For them, all that matters
Is their *'respectable'* positions within society
<u>Yes, that's all that matters!</u>

Awful consequences may flow
From the stroke of a pen
When a signature is used
To legitimize a state-based evil

UNITY

Give us unity Lord
The right kind of unity
A unity – not of compromise
But of compassion
A unity based upon
Your truth
Your Spirit
And your love
Amen

UNLEASHED

The wrath of Yahweh has erupted with violence
It is overwhelmingly awesome and powerful
Fierce and terrible
Great and limitless
It crushes all before it!

It is worse than the explosion of ...
A thousand volcanoes
A million solar flares
A billion supernovas
It vaporises all before it!

A Spirit of confusion has been unleashed
On
        a
                faithless
                              hierarchy
who
        have
                wilfully
                            placed
Their
        own
                selfish
                            interests
above
        God's
                Revealed
                          Truth.

Babylon cannot be healed (Jeremiah 51:9)

The Anglican Communion (((sways)))
                                          And
                            (((totters)))
Like
        an
                inebriated old whore
        Drunk on spirits and liquor
                She has foolishly consumed

The appointment of
A
       Merlin Archbishop
Has unleashed
         chaos
PANDEMONIUM now reigns
Amongst
A disobedient leadership
       Who have shown contempt

For the divine Word
And scorn
      For an
        Old Covenant people.
They drink from a cup of wrath
A cup of divine wrath
This causes them
       to flout their sins in full public view

Beneath a heavenly altar
'Bloody Mary's' martyrs[26]
         Cry out
"How long, O Lord, how long
Will you allow your sacrifice to be mocked
By liars who blaspheme your name?
When, oh when will You act?"

But on earth below
Bishop bullies Bishop
Clergy clash with clergy
Fanatic fights fanatic
And
A multitude of factions vie for supremacy
The zealous are consumed by hatred
The reasonable are consumed by despair
And the Devil is consumed with glee.
Under the tyranny of scoffers
The love of many has grown cold
Christ's words in Matthew 24:10-12

---

[26] A reference to the (approximately) three hundred Protestants under the reign of Mary Tudor (1553-1558) and known as *'Bloody Mary.'*

Have assumed a terrible fulfilment
A whole communion is under divine WRATH

But still
        Many congregations remain oblivious
To the terrible judgement
>>> Hurtling toward them
With the raging fury of a melting, molten lava flow
Or the sheer terror of a Tsunami Tidal wave
Decimating all before it
These people are lost in stupor
As their leaders dart aimlessly
From one crisis conference to another –
Not knowing what to do

In Heaven
Millions of Angels and Saints
Wait with bated breath.
They listen in hushed silence
As, from God's royal throne
A solemn announcement is soon to be made:
The Father says to the Son:
"This is a body of people
In whom I have no pleasure
They have made themselves accursed
By spurning my Word
They have clearly revealed
The full measure of their antagonism
By turning against my people, Israel"
In loving reverence the Son replies:
"A loyal remnant must be created,
Let us send the Spirit to accomplish this task"
For only He can retrieve matters"

In loving reverence the Spirit responds to the Father:
"This work will be accomplished
Through painful anguish,
For there are many in the Anglican Communion
Who resist your truth and hate your Word
Even the best of them
Will need to be forcibly weaned from their idols"

"Let this be so," the Father responds
"GO FORTH AND CREATE."

On Earth, beleaguered Saints weep bitterly, crying out
"Who can be saved?
What can be done?
Where will we go?
Will God be merciful?
Despair opens up like a yawning chasm
All is lost, utterly lost
All hope is gone
All confidence crushed
Where can we run to?
And where can we flee?
Persecution is now our lot!"

From Heaven, the Spirit replies: -
"Hush and hear, you distressed children of God
Take heed and listen you confused sons of the Father
Be faithful unto death.
You have neither been forsaken nor abandoned
A holy blood covers your sins
But BE ALERT and realise that …
Now is the time for urgent prayer
Now is the time for creative thinking
Now is the time for making a bold stand
And for drawing close to Jesus -
The Word made flesh
The ONLY effective Mediator
Between Man and God.
Witness faithfully to the Gospel
And you WILL be rewarded."

"Dear God,
Amidst wrath remember mercy
In this hour of darkness
Please protect and preserve
Those who REALLY belong to you
And grant them the strength and the opportunity
To share your Holy Gospel
For the glory of your great and marvellous Name,
Let this be so, Amen."

WHAT MADNESS?

Questions

What madness is this which defiles the sacrament of love?

What madness is this which profanes Holy Communion?

What madness is this which mocks the very name of God By comforting the deluded in the corruption of their ways?

Answers

It is a madness which springs from the pride of men

It is a madness which comes from those who *'affirm'* a lie

It is a madness which arises from those whose wills
Are locked in mortal combat with the Word of God

Questions

Is it a madness which can be cured by the Father's mercy?

Is it a madness able to be healed by the Son's compassion?

Is it a madness which can be calmed by the grace of God's gentle Spirit?

Answers

No, it is a madness which cannot be healed
For the Father's mercy has been scorned

No, it is a madness which cannot be cured
For the Son's compassion has been snubbed

No, it is a madness which cannot be calmed
For the Spirit's grace has been spurned
By those given over to their own reprobate hearts

WITHDRAWAL

God's Spirit has withdrawn

Leaving many in the Church
To follow their own devices

God's Spirit has withdrawn

Leaving many in the Church
To die in their sins

God's Spirit has withdrawn

Leaving many in the Church
To the darkness and futility of their own minds

God's Spirit has withdrawn

Leaving many in the Church
To pursue their own selfish desires

God's Spirit has withdrawn

Leaving many in the Church
To languish in wilful deception

God's Spirit has withdrawn

Leaving many in the Church
To follow the idols of their own hearts

God's Spirit has withdrawn

Leaving many in the Church
To indulge in long-cherished lusts

God's Spirit has withdrawn

Leaving many in the Church
To wallow in their own filth

God's Spirit has withdrawn

Leaving many in the Church
To be swept away by bitter hatred

God's Spirit has withdrawn

Leaving many in the Church
To abuse those in their care

God's Spirit has withdrawn

Leaving many in the Church
To be moulded by an amoral society

God's Spirit has withdrawn

Leaving many in the Church
To grope blindly in spiritual darkness

God's Spirit has withdrawn

Leaving many in the Church
To be seduced by Lucifer's delusions

God's Spirit has withdrawn

Leaving many in the Church
To be filled with demons

God's Spirit has withdrawn

Leaving many in the Church
To perish forever in the raging fires of Hell

YOU WERE

As a Church you were born in fornication
Your origins lay in the lusts of a King[27]
Like your mother before you[28]
You began practising your harlotries from an early age
With hasty recklessness
You made a strange bedfellow
With Renaissance Humanism
And the worst aspects of Catholicism
The State was your pimp
And its orders you gladly obeyed.

As you began to grow
You seized other lovers
Ejecting from your house
Those who protested at your behaviour[29]
Oppression was your garment
And avarice your jewellery –
Of mercy you knew nothing

In middle age you became fat and lazy[30]
Yet the Lord remembered those martyred
By a bloodthirsty queen[31]
In His patience He sent you revival –
Raising up godly leaders[32]
To show you the truth
And enable you to take His Gospel
To the ends of the earth[33]

---

[27] A reference to King Henry VIII's lust for his mistress (and subsequent wife) Anne Boleyn (1501-1536) which helped set off the English Reformation during the 1530s
[28] A reference to the Medieval Roman Catholic Church
[29] A reference to the expulsion of Puritan Clergy in 1662
[30] A reference to the Church of England during the eighteenth century
[31] A reference to Protestant martyrs, killed under Mary Tudor (1553-1558)
[32] A reference to the eighteenth-century revivals under the leadership of the Wesley brothers and John Whitfield
[33] A reference to the Missionary Movements, resulting from the eighteenth-century revivals

But in your flippant smugness
You resisted the Holy Spirit's wooing
Choosing to remain unfaithful
To the One who had courted you with love
In brazen defiance
You flirted once more
With the repugnant superstitions of Rome[34]
As well as the futile vanities of Liberalism
But your favourite idol was *'respectability'*
High social status became your God[35]
You conceived many illegitimate children
Who repeated your harlotries[36]

Yet, in His graciousness
The Lord spared you foreign invasion.
Spain, France and Germany
Were all held back by His outstretched arm.
Kings and dictators alike sought in vain
To cross over to your shores

As you entered a decrepit old age
You still practised your harlotries
With the base children of twentieth century unbelief[37]
Attempts to apply layers of make-up
And to speak in a refined lady-like voice
Failed to hide your decay.[38]

In time you became hideous and diseased
Like an impoverished old crone
You leapt into bed with every wayfarer

---

[34] A reference to flamboyant forms of early Anglo-Catholicism, associated with the nineteenth century *'Oxford Movement'*
[35] A reference to the Church of England during the nineteenth and early twentieth centuries
[36] A reference to breakaway movements (like Methodism) which had formerly been associated with the Church of England. Despite a very good start it would replicate the apostasy of its *'mother church.'*
[37] A reference to Marxist, Freudian and Existential philosophies – all of which are based upon Atheistic Humanism
[38] A reference to the many futile attempts by the Church of England to gain a favourable public image. This could be seen in such initiatives as (the now long forgotten) 1985 report *'Faith in the City'* that annoyed the then prime minister Margaret Thatcher for its apparent Marxist leanings.

Who happened to pass by,
In a desperate frenzy you pleaded
'Fulfil my desires and give me new life!'
Alcoholic tramps became your lovers
And poisoned needles your payment[39]
You sought comfort in dark areas
Forbidden by God's Word[40]
You even tried to opportune
Members of other faiths to be your lovers
And you renewed your flirtation with Rome[41]

Yet, in His mercy
The Lord withheld His judgements
Hoping that, even at this late stage
You would respond to His love
And honour the One who died for you.
From His Spirit came renewal
And more Godly leaders were raised up
To minister to you;[42]
Because you were weak
The Lord spoke to you gently
Refusing to give you over
To either Communism or to Nuclear War
<u>But still you failed to respond</u>

With suicidal defiance
You persisted in your prostitutions
Ignoring the warnings given to you.
A shrug of the shoulders
And a complacent smile was your only response.
You made a mockery of God's Spirit
When you drank poisoned wine from Toronto
Turning His gifts into an absurdity[43]
A Druid became your latest husband[44]

---

[39] A reference to the destructive Secular Humanist influences the Church of England picked-up during the 1960s.
[40] A reference to the widespread practice of Freemasonry and Spiritualism from the Victorian age to the present time.
[41] A reference to the Interfaith and Ecumenical Movements
[42] A reference to leaders like David Watson (1933-1984)
[43] A reference to the *'Toronto Experience'* and its associated excesses
[44] A reference to the appointment of Dr Rowan Williams, enthroned as Archbishop of Canterbury, in February 2003.

With eagerness you embraced him
Glibly accepting his seductions
Whilst still refusing to acknowledge
Your own plight!

In your decrepitude you have become
Blind, deaf and incontinent
Discharging fluids which threaten to cause disease
The stench you give is noxious
But still you grope after new lovers

Yet, in His compassion
The Lord gave you many chances to repent
From the *'Global South'*[45] he raised-up witnesses
To confront you with the truth
They were men
With no respect for religious pretension –
<u>But still you did not respond</u>

He continues to confront you with your iniquity.
But even in this late hour
You <u>will not listen</u>
For the things of God
Have become unimportant to you

Now the Lord is weary of your endless lustful affairs
You have incensed Him with your harlotries
Your feeble excuses have become tiresome
And tedious in the extreme
Already, His judgements have begun
Division is now your lot
And soon your disease-ridden nakedness
Will be exposed for all to see
The lovers you craved for will desert you
Destitution will be your lot
A gang of psychotic murderers
Will tear you apart
Those you flirted with will torture you

---

[45] A reference to various African prelates who challenged the doctrinal and moral decline in bodies like the Church of England during the late twentieth and early twenty-first centuries.

Endless humiliation will be your fate!
Yet even then your only response
Will be to wiggle your arthritic hips
And blow kisses to a *'New World Order'*
You will go on seeking new lovers
Until the bitter end

Oh, Church of England, the Lord Himself
Is arrayed against you
There will be no refuge
From His all-consuming wrath
But still you do not see this
For you have been faithless and blind to His Word

End Notes

Dates following the title show when each piece was first drafted.
Alas: Saturday, 28th March 2009
Anglican Agony: Sunday, 29th May 2005. It explores the way God can still work through the chaos of His Church.
Bishop of Sin: Friday, 13th June 2003. It uses a fictitious character to satirize the corrupt attitudes of many senior leaders in the Church of England. It was influenced by C. S. Lewis' portrayal of the *'Episcopal Ghost'* in his book *'The Great Divorce.'*
How Dare They? Monday, 20th May 2008. It expresses the anger I felt on hearing that Senior Traditionalists at the (then forthcoming) Lambeth Conference (which took place the following July) were willing to celebrate the Eucharist with militantly apostate Bishops. The latter had wilfully endorsed a variety of doctrinal errors and immoral practices.
How Many? Wednesday, 28th September 2005. It was written during a time of controversy concerning the future of the Anglican Communion. It expresses how senior Anglican figures were willing to consider <u>every other option</u> apart from that of following Jesus Christ.
New Age Woman: Friday, 22nd March 2013
Ritual Defilement: Wednesday, 19th September 2007. It expresses the horror I feel whenever the Eucharist is misused to serve political ends, e.g. promoting a non-existent unity
Small Ambitions: Friday, 27th July 2012

The Answer: Wednesday, 28th September 2005 when musing over the degeneration of the Episcopalian Church of America. It expresses the way unbelief gets the Church into a mess. Whilst writing it I kept hearing the words from Bob Dylan's song *'Blowing In the Wind.'*
The Stroke of a Pen: Monday, 25th June 2018
Unity: Wednesday, 4th October 1989. It was a prayer (made in public) during a period of open intercession at a Christian Conference held in Scotland. It expresses the need to ask God to give His people <u>the right kind of unity</u> in the face of growing deception within the Church.
Unleashed: Thursday, 30th June 2005. Written in response to the vain political manoeuvrings of the Anglican Consultative Council (held in Nottingham, from Sunday, 19th to Tuesday, 28th June 2005). Its emphasises the need to hope in God amidst His judgement of the Anglican Communion. Stylistically, it represents one of my most ambitious pieces.
What Madness! Wednesday, 19th September 2007
Withdrawal: Saturday, 11th September 2004. In the original version the words *'in the Church'* read as *'Anglicans.'* The change was made to broaden its application.
You Were: Thursday, 4th March 1993 (and slightly modified in February 2004 when it had become clear that its contents were more relevant than ever before.) It underlines <u>the persistent presence of apostasy within the Anglican Communion.</u> It was last updated in March 2019.

The most pathetic grouping present within the Church of England were the Establishment Evangelicals who misguidedly clung onto their membership despite the growing corruption. Mainly drawn from the professional classes, they were only *'Evangelical'* up to when it risked getting them excluded from that body. Generally, they behaved like a wife unwilling to leave an abusive husband. A lack of courage and a desire to preserve an imaginary respectability was responsible for this disastrous stance. The pressure group tactics practiced by the defunct Reform organization (1993-2018) and the Church Society achieved nothing of substance. Their strategy of trying to change things by remaining within the Church of England proved an abject failure.

ACT 3: THE CATASTROPHE

SCENE 1: THE WASTELANDS

Zephaniah 1:15, *"That day is a day of wrath, a day of trouble and distress, a day of waste and desolation, a day of darkness and gloominess, a day of clouds and thick darkness."*

A PLEA FOR DELIVERANCE

Do not remain silent, Oh Lord
Do not stand aside, Oh Christ
Do not remain hidden, Oh Lord
Hurry! Intervene! Speak!
Show me what I should do
Guide me into the way I should go
Lead me into pastures new
And bless me – as you did in former days

Let not my strength dwindle to nothing
Let not my talents go to waste
Let not my abilities wither away
Embolden me with your Spirit
For Yahweh – you are my God and my Lord!
Yeshua, your Son, is my only Saviour
Immerse me in your love
Flood me with your grace
Cover me with your mercy
So that I may be an effective witness
To those to whom you send me

Please do not tarry
Please do not delay
Please do not wait
Let not my confidence
Melt away like wax
Act now, oh God
Lest I perish
And defame your Holy Name!

MEMORIAL CITIES

STRICTLY CONFIDENTIAL

THIS DOCUMENT IS FOR LIMITED CIRCULATION ONLY

ANY UNAUTHORISED REPRODUCTION WILL RESULT IN LEGAL ACTION BEING TAKEN – ON THE BASIS OF CLAUSE 13.6 OF THE NEW GLOBAL COPYRIGHT ACT. MAXIMUN PENALTY, TWENTY-FIVE YEARS IMPRISONMENT

DRAFT REPORT OUTLINE

(STRICTLY CONFIDENTIAL, NO UNAUTHORISED REPRODUCTION PERMITTED)

Containing Figures FAO The Senior Global Reconstruction Commission (Middle Eastern, Central Asian and North African Regions)

Please forward to the Global Official Directorship (GOD)

Memorial City 1
(Former capital city of..)
Dead 6,000,000
(Margin of error[46] 3%)
No known survivors
Status: uninhabitable

Memorial City 2
(Former capital city of..)
Dead 2,000,000
(Margin of error 3%)
No known survivors
Status: uninhabitable

---

[46] A *'margin of error'* is a statistical term meaning that the figure could be 180,000 either way of 6,000,000. The figure of 180,000 being 3% of 6,000,000.

Memorial City 3
(Former capital city of..)
Dead 13,000,000
(Margin of error 5%)
13 survived for two weeks
11 subsequently died from radiation sickness
Status: uninhabitable

Memorial City 101
(Formerly known as..)
Dead 1,600,000
(Margin of error 3%)
No known survivors
Status: uninhabitable

Memorial City 102
(Formerly known as..)
Dead 1,500,000
(Margin of error 5%)
2 survived
1 subsequently committed suicide
Status: uninhabitable

Memorial City 103
(Formerly known as..)
Dead 3,600,000
(Margin of error 4%)
150 survived
132 subsequently died from radiation sickness
Status: suburbs now partly inhabitable

Estimated Totals

Number of dead 600,000,000
(Margin of error 3.5%)

Number of survivors: under 100,000,
(Precise figures as yet unavailable)

Estimated proportion of land rendered permanently uninhabitable 6%

Estimated proportion of land rendered currently uninhabitable 13%(Severe risk of radiation sickness)

Estimated proportion of land rendered partly uninhabitable 20% (Some risk of radiation sickness)

Proportion of land cleared of radiation 0.03%
(Mainly transport networks and natural resource centres)

Level of Biochemical Contamination: As yet unknown

Estimated loss of Gross Domestic Product 90%

Estimated loss of oil production 81%

Estimated loss of agricultural production 65%

Regional food and fuel reserves: Nil

Long term re-settlement prospects: poor

Long term oil extraction prospects: variable

Refugee problem: Severe but will reduce as the number of survivors decline through natural wastage caused by the effect of radiation and deprivation of basic necessities.

The above estimates may be revised as further data is obtained from both aerial and satellite observation. Land surveys are currently only possible within narrowly defined areas.

Draft proposal

The Commission should continue to give priority to restoring basic communication infrastructure and natural energy supplies. Funding (if available) is to be confined to those survivors having the required skills to assist in the above priority. A provisional estimate would suggest between 700-900 known such survivors.

The geo-strategic location of Memorial Cities 1 and 2 would suggest that, in the long term, their outer suburbs could be visited by foreign tourists as long as strict decontamination procedures are observed. Brief over-flight visits, spanning their central craters should further enhance commercial revenue (as would visits made by those with former family connections).

In the very long term, these sites may provide dramatic settings for film production or historical reconstructions. Should the level of contamination remain high then alternative sites must be located.

Until extensive decontamination takes place the precise real estate values are impossible to estimate.

A Memorial Book is to be produced − with any subsequent profits used to cover administrative costs.

A Public Relations Firm must be hired to encourage public acceptance of controversial decisions. A caring image must be consistently communicated.

Due to the sensitivities involved, further discussion of this draft proposal is strongly recommended. Current financial constraints may hinder implementation.

However, scope still exists for the GOD to pursue the agenda of implementing a robust One World Order. The latest Quantum Computer Models suggest the validity of this option. The economic, environmental and political turbulence resulting from the recent conflict should generate a robust demand from key cultural influencers to promote this highly progressive aim.

It is therefore strongly recommended that this option be explored by *'The Truth and Reconciliation Department'* with immediate effect.

NUCLEAR SORROWS

Cry, howl, weep, for the fiery destruction
Which will befall many in the Middle East and elsewhere

Grieve, heave, sob, for its many inhabitants
Who will be incinerated into fine, powdery ash

Groan, moan, mourn for those unborn infants and children
Who will never live to enjoy adulthood

Lament noisily for a region in the world
Destroyed by those engaged in the politics of hatred.
Whole nations martyred in the name of faith

Piles of broken, smashed rubble
Choking, eye-stinging dust
Billowing, filthy brown smoke
Scurrying, panicking, fleeing figures
Hurrying like scattered ants
Across a landscape of death

Mass destruction has reached our shores
Because of those political extremists who boasted
'We are all Hezbollah now!'
'Sieg Heil! Sieg Heil! Sieg Heil!...

PRESERVE US

Preserve us from enduring
A serious worsening of world conditions

Preserve us from enduring
The rise of the anti-Christ and his false prophet

Preserve us from enduring
Their seduction of all of the nations

Preserve us from enduring
Their attempt to kill every Christian and Jew

Preserve us from enduring
The murderous fury of 'The Great Tribulation'

Preserve us from enduring
The searing heat caused by climate change

Preserve us from enduring
The sight of a looming mushroom cloud

Preserve us from enduring
The complete devastation of the whole earth

Preserve us from enduring
The virtual destruction of the human race

If, good Lord
You preserve my wife and I
From having to endure these afflictions
You will have been truly merciful
And we will have been greatly blest

SEEING

What do I see?

A landscape of burnt heather and blackened, scorched earth

So shall be the cities of those who hate God's people

What do I see?

Burnt twisted stubble and dark powdered ash

So shall be the corpses of those who hate God's people

What do I see?

Cracked and fired sandstone lying amidst the stubble

So shall be the bones of those who hate God's people

What do I see?

A handful of hungry sheep desperately gnawing at the ground

So shall be the few survivors of those who hate God's people

What do I see?

Murky clouds mushrooming over the horizon

So shall be the nuclear fate of those who hate God's people

STORM WARNING

Just as the gales
Which swept our land
Appeared endless in their duration
So shall be the tribulation
To be sent upon this country

Just as houses shook and rattled
Under the blow of fierce gales
So shall all of the institutions in this country
Be shaken to their very foundations

Just as you gaped, open-mouthed
At uprooted trees flung over an open road
So shall the Lord throw down
All those structures which hinder His Spirit

Just as you tentatively
Walked around fallen slates
Which lay scattered about
So shall God's people bypass
The deceptions spread by false teachers

Just as you ducked the litter
Which whirled around in fierce gusts of wind
So shall you learn to avoid
The dangerous temptations of this world

Just as you stared incredulously
At the tumbled-down walls
So shall you see the Lord
Ruin the works of those
Who erect walls against His Spirit

Just as you heard people
Wondering at what was happening
So shall the coming tribulation
Compel people to question
Their most basic values

Pay heed to the gales
Sent earlier this year
They were the Lord's *'storm warning'*
To both the UK and the world

Yes! He is the one true God
Who speaks through
The most violent forces of nature
Gales, storms and hurricanes
Are the breath of His mouth

THE ABORTION OF HOPE

Part 1: Hope Lost

When I look ahead
I foresee a looming catastrophe
Producing endless misery

I wish I knew what to say
But our society has lost its way
Mountainous debts it can no longer repay

Gadarene bankers are unwilling to lend
It's all coming to a messy end
Is there anything left to mend?

The whole world's capital begins to fly
Causing Western economies to wane and die
As lower interest rates are given *'just one more try'*

The monetary system is threatening to crash
Inevitably ending in a gruesome *'big smash'*
With banking bonds thrown aside as so much trash

Many businesses plunge deep into the red
Their owners wishing they were dead
But all having to stand and face it instead

The mantle of glory has blown to the East
Hardworking Asians enjoy many a feast
Western aspirations have now largely ceased

There a light-speed techno revolution
Battering against every major institution
But will it offer any real solution?

Communism's promise of a workers' utopia
Produced nothing but a grim dystopia
And from progressive intellectuals a craven myopia

The offer of freedom for the proletariat
Gave birth to a bureaucratic secretariat
With no-one quite knowing *'where they were at!'*

The promise of State Socialism – so easy to swallow
Yet disappointingly proving itself so hollow
Inevitably bringing nothing but sorrow

The worst vices of Ancient Rome
Are carelessly beamed into every home
Feeding the excesses to which we're already prone

Puffed-up celebrities, full of shallow pretence
Behave so bizarrely – it makes very little sense
As they parade on TV, looking utterly dense

A person sits in front of a computer screen
But all is not what it may seem
A message flashes-up showing a dubious theme

Cyber images prance and dance
Some offering a large financial advance
Ensnaring users in a deceptive stance

Facebook has become a mighty hook
To advertisers it's a *'let's open and look'*
Giving a *'respectable'* cover to many a crook

We're riders on the storm
Where cruelty's the norm
And the arts have lost their form

Some, in God's name, wish to maim and kill
Mass murder giving them a heart-stopping thrill
Others want the elderly to take a fatal poison pill

No mourners attend the death of Theology
It's now been replaced by a glib Semiology
(That's a branch of linguistic Sociology)

Oh the horror! Oh the horror!
Our land has turned into a desolate Gomorrah
In which there can be no *'tomorrow'*

Right is wrong and wrong is right
Slighted reason has taken flight
And all that's left is not a pretty sight!

I look around, fear clutching at my heart
Forlornly wishing I could just depart
Or be given time to make a fresh start

There's nowhere left to run and hide
An abundance of hatred incessantly supplied
With narcotic escapes terminally applied

The crime of embryocide
Was an undercover infanticide
It led to assisted suicide

That escalated into mass homicide
And a most cruel genocide
All resulting from Man's deicide
Which itself is a crime of regicide

With God supposedly *'dead'*
Humanity completely *'lost its head'*
And to ever-present evil was gladly wed

Fools laugh and dance their merry way to Hell
Both body and soul they gladly sell
For what rational reason, I cannot tell

For many, leisure is only a trifling pleasure
They overlook how it's a definite treasure
But coming at a cost no one wants to measure

Present is an abortion of hope
With many frying their heads on dope
As daily life leaves them unable to cope

They stumble in blind confusion
With an underlying fear of nuclear fusion
Leading to radioactive dissolution

Our society stands on the eve of destruction
So many failed attempts at social construction
Which ended only in violent eruption

The masters of War see their profits soar
But greedily they want more, more, more!
As the blood of all others continues to outpour

The universal soldier is a boy of ten
Kidnapped at the age of seven
And drugged into the killing of men

My courage begins to fail
I turn a whiter shade of pale
And my arms begin to flail

I get only bad vibrations
When future decimations
Form the subject of my contemplations

I could shout aloud and vigorously protest
And even risk my own arrest
Is there no ease to my distress?

In the year 2525
Will anyone be left alive
Can anyone survive?

Churches have long-since betrayed their Lord
With the truth they became apathetically bored
Well-nigh oblivious to His judgemental sword

Another false answer is blowing in the wind
With praises to a pseudo-Messiah, noisily hymned
Totally ignoring the fact that we all have sinned

This Messiah-man promises that we <u>can</u> overcome
For all of humanity belongs to the *'cosmic one'*
With every nation prostrating themselves under <u>his</u> thumb

In desperation many shall believe his lie
Because it provides such a wonderful *'high'*
Yet in trusting its false promises <u>many will die</u>

My despair seems beyond repair
To the future I dare no longer stare
It seems so unfair – why should I even care?

Part 2: Hope Restored

My patience has worn very thin
The light of faith barely flickering and dim
But in brokenness I turn to Him

As evil sweeps in like a raging flood
Covering all with much-polluted mud
I trust in His atoning blood

Can it be that His amazing grace
Has saved me and taken despair from my face
Securing for me a heavenly place?

Yes – assuredly I am His
My heart is full of peaceful bliss
His will I'll endeavour never to miss

For my cancerous sins He paid the price
Completed in His sacrifice!
His presence more than does suffice!

I may be something of a clod
But a *'mighty fortress'* is my God
I couldn't care if others find that odd

When I peer wistfully toward eternity
I know, Jesus, you're my only certainty
You belong to that Blessèd Trinity

With you I will dwell
Having been spared the fires of Hell
What a story I have to tell!

So wonderfully great thou art
Thanks for giving me a brand-new start
Let me now begin to play my part

For to dwell in You is to dwell in light
You've saved me by your powerful might
Oh Jesus, you are my first delight!

Come all you faithful
Show how much you're grateful
By being wholeheartedly worshipful!

THE NATIONS HISS

Like boiling water in a pan
The nations bubble
The nations hiss
The nations seethe
The nations writhe

Yes, the nations are in turmoil
All have turned against God's people-Israel
An irrational hatred guides their every action
As united they stand in global rebellion
Against the Lord, who created them

But like criminals sentenced to the gallows
Their destruction is near
The punishment of these nations cannot be deferred
Their time has run out
Their executioner awaits
Soon He will act

Armed masses gather in the land
Amidst the din of battle
Mighty military hordes struggle
No mercy is shown
Clouds of choking dust cover the scene

The noise of war is heard from far away
Its clamour reverberates in every nation
The world watches in suspense
Many pray to their various gods
But the annihilation of false religion draws near

In an instance of time
God will save His chosen ones
Many will perish
But those who remain
Will be a testimony to the whole world
For He is faithful to all of His covenant promises
Once made to Abraham

End Notes

Dates following the title show when each piece was first drafted.

Lest! Saturday, 12th March 2016

Memorial cities: Monday, 15th October 2007. It expresses the likely destructive consequences of the hatreds currently raging in the Middle East. The final paragraph was first drafted on Wednesday, 10th October 2018 and inserted on Monday, 25th March 2019. By then, there had been a partial fulfilment of this scenario through the use of conventional weapons in countries like Syria.

Nuclear Sorrows: Monday, 18th September 2006. First drafted in the mid-afternoon near the ridge of a certain Moor. It expresses my emotions concerning about the rising tide of violent religious-political fanaticism in the Middle East and elsewhere in the world

Preserve us: Sunday, 18th May 2019

Seeing: Penned in the late afternoon of Monday, 18th September 2006. I was standing near some charred ground in front of a walled coniferous tree plantation. At the time, I felt as though I was in a time portal, subjectively viewing the remains of a Middle Eastern City in the not too distant future.

Storm Warning: Thursday, 13th June 1990. Written when beginning a prayer retreat, this poem explores how God can speak through the natural forces in His Creation. (The weather at the beginning of 1990 had been characterized by severe gales.)

The Abortion of Hope: Sunday, 28th November 2010; the last verse added on Saturday 9th April 2011.

The Nations Hiss: Friday, 24th January 1992. This poem emphasises how the Lord will rescue a remnant of Jewish people in Israel. This will take place during a time of armed conflict, when each of the world's nations will be arrayed against Israel.

SCENE 2: THE SURVIVORS

Lamentations 2:14, *"Your prophets have seen vain and foolish things for you: and they have not discovered your iniquity nor averted your captivity* [by leading you to repentance] *but have seen for you false prophecies that have caused your banishment."*

DEFEATED

I went confidently into battle
But you, Lord, were not with me

I repeatedly attacked the same stronghold
(Again and again I went forward)
But you, Lord, gave me over to defeat

I clung on, despite endless setbacks
But you, Lord, forced me to retreat

I persevered, refusing to give in
But you, Lord, brought bitter humiliation

I frequently cried out for your help
But you, Lord, turned a deaf ear

I pleaded for your assistance
But you, Lord, left me defenceless
(Against a bitter enemy, you left me defenceless!)

Feverishly, I wondered what had gone so wrong – and why
But you, Lord, abandoned me to confusion

And now my strength has all but gone
Is it not time for you to act?

FILL

Lord, in this time of trial
Fill us with your grace and love
Fill us with your joy and peace
Fill us with your patience and gentleness
Fill us with your goodness and faith
Fill us with your humility and meekness
Fill us with your strength and self-control
Fill us with your wisdom and courage
So that we may <u>boldly proclaim</u>
That Jesus, your Son
Is the <u>only Saviour of the World!</u>

FOG

Oh, sweet Lord Jesus
Please help me
For I am lost
Lost in a spiritual fog
Where can I go?
What can I do?
For I am lost
Lost in an impenetrable spiritual fog

LEGACY

Should I be killed
Let this be my prayer
That my death will result
In the Gospel spreading rapidly
Amongst Jewish and Asian people
So that a worthwhile legacy
Will have been left behind

May this be for the glory
Of God my Father
And of His Son, my Saviour
The Lord Jesus Christ, Amen

PRIDE

Good Lord Jesus
Preserve your servant
From all overbearing pride
In future, help me to boast only of you
And not of myself, Amen

RELATING TO JESUS

The faithful believer treats Jesus as *'Friend'*
The spiritual believer treats Jesus as *'God'*
The industrious believer treats Jesus as *'Co-Worker'*
The passionate believer treats Jesus as *'Lover'*
The fearful believer treats Jesus as *'Daddy'*
The needy believer treats Jesus as *'Doctor'*
The embattled believer treats Jesus as *'Soldier'*
The political believer treats Jesus as *'Co-conspirator'*
The ambitious believer treats Jesus as *'Business Partner'*

No matter <u>how</u> you relate to Him, <u>always be open and honest in your relationship with Him.</u> Take care to follow His will once it has been clearly discerned.

RELIEF

The storm is over
The hurricane has passed
The deluge has ebbed
Our land is now at peace

The sea is calm
The waves break softly
The whirlpools have gone
And the treacherous eddies flow no more

The fear has evaporated
The panic now ceased
The clamour has died away
And the dread has all but gone

The trial is over
Thank God we live

STAND STILL

Stand still
Do not move
Rest in His presence
Recover your strength –
Before engaging in endless activities

Then Jesus will refresh you
And prepare you for future service

Already the doors of opportunity have opened
But wait before you enter them
Lest exhaustion cause you
To make many needless errors

SWEEP IN

Oh, Heavenly Father,
Sweep in with your Holy Spirit
Let Pentecost blessings fall afresh
Stir up my talents
Use them to your glory
Take my abilities to their limit
Strengthen me with your grace
And please help me
To gain a clearer vision
Of your Son, the Lord Jesus Christ

Please answer this prayer
For the sake of Your great
And Holy Name, Amen

THEY PROMISED

"God wants you rich!"
So they asserted

"Receive this word of knowledge!"
So they advised

"Enjoy the fullness of blessing!"
So they counselled

"Realize your full potential!"
So they encouraged

"'Name and claim' your blessing!"
So they exhorted

"'Come out of your mind' and 'go with the flow!"
So they nagged

"Don't analyse, just receive the blessing!"
So they pressurised

"You can have a life of flourishing abundance!"
So they promised

"You are the King's kids!"
So they asserted

"Be part of God's mighty army!"
So they shouted

"God is doing a new thing!"
So they stated

"Exercise the power of faith, faith, faith and claim your miracle!"
So they yelled

"Touch not the Lord's anointed!"
So they threatened

With itching ears
We eagerly heeded them
Rushing forward in meeting after meeting
To receive a *'special anointing'*
Every word they uttered
We treated as *'gospel'* –
As a revelation of the divine.
We were so confident
After all – this was God's *'party time!'*
Revival was guaranteed
And a whole myriad of miracles
Would soon confound the doubters

We were the *'manifest sons of God!'*
The *'new breed'* of believers
Members of *'Joel's army'* –
Capturing territory for the Lord –
And ruling all the nations for Him!
Our sole purpose
Was to get the world ready
For Jesus' return!

Dominion was ours
And we had the right to exercise it.
As the new *'Masters of the Universe'*
Our power had no limits
"Revelation knowledge"
Was ours for the taking
Our initiation into *"deeper mysteries"*
Transported us to *"a higher plain of spirituality
Where we could communicate with angels!"*
Our eyes were opened
We would not die
But be like gods
Knowing the difference between good and evil!

But –

They promised us a blessing
We got cursing

They promised us wealth

We got poverty

They promised us health
We got sickness

They promised us abundance
We got hunger

They promised us success
We got failure

They promised us victory
We got defeat

They promised us peace
We got war

They promised us strength
We got weakness

They promised us laughter
We got tears

They promised us joy
We got misery

They promised us light
We got darkness

They promised us revelation
We got confusion

They promised us life
We got death

They promised us everything
But in the end
We got nothing
But disillusionment, destitution and despair

Surely –
We are a betrayed generation
Directionless, purposeless and lost
Failure, oppression and poverty
Is now our only lot
What we thought of as faith
Was nothing more than an enticing illusion
We had exalted ourselves in the place of God

Consequently –

Instead of being *'filled'*
We were left empty

Instead of being *'set free'*
We were left in bondage

Instead of being *'delivered'*
We were left enslaved

Instead of being *'blessed with flourishing prosperity'*
We were cursed with frustrating poverty

Now –

A crushing sense of shame haunts us
Our savings have all but gone
And we don't know
Where our next meal is coming from
Financially, we're ruined
We can't meet our bills
Nor can we repay our debts
Our marriages are breaking-up
And we're losing our homes
Our children go hungry because of our poverty
An overwhelming sense of desolation
Weighs down heavily upon us
All our hope is gone
Bailiffs hammer on the door
Noisily demanding an entrance
So they can evict us out onto the street
A terrible reckoning has befallen us

Yet it seems so unfair
That our children should suffer too
We're even pawning their toys
To help us *'pay our way,'*
Dependent upon the cold charity of others
We feel totally dejected, humiliated and crushed
Many of us are sick through stress
Oh, how eager we were
To follow the preachers of prosperity
The <u>great liars</u> of our time –
Whose faith was nothing more than proud foolishness!
Whose testimonies consisted of hollow, empty boasts!
How we hung upon their every word
Oh, <u>the time we wasted</u> in their endless meetings
How greedily we gulped-down their poisoned *'new wine!'*

As a people we loved stupidity
We showed this
By plunging into *'rivers of blessing'*
Unaware that their filthy and polluted waters
Would sweep us into a vortex of ruin

Our places of worship
Became theatres of depravity

Only now has the realization dawned
That power-hungry dictators were our apostles
Frenzied witchdoctors our prophets
Loud entertainers our evangelists
Sly manipulators our pastors
And boastful egotists our teachers
These were the people
We willingly placed upon high pedestals
Of power and grandeur
How we loved their boastful testimonies and winsome smiles
After all – <u>they made us feel good!</u>
We happily handed over our hard-earned money
Laughing uproariously as we did so
In our vain hope of receiving it back at some future date
Surely God would *'multiply our seed of faith'*
And we would be rich, rich, rich!
After all, wasn't poverty a sign that we lacked faith in Him?

How frivolously entertained we were by their preaching
How they added sparkle to our dull and dreary lives
How we convulsed with laughter at their antics
Swooning on the floor in response to their hypnotic suggestions
We would often hear them yell *"Let the fire fall!"* –
Totally unaware that it was a fire of judgement
They were invoking

We believed in them
Because they told us
What we wanted to hear
We desperately clung to their lying fantasies
Willing them to be
True visions of God

Indeed –

We were so readily won over
By their promises of easy wealth
That we applauded their acts
We cheered their claims
We laughed at their jokes
We even waved colourful banners
In their *'celebration meetings'*

But we were fooled
Because we had first fooled ourselves
We believed that God
Would grant our every selfish wish and whim
All we ever needed to do
Was to apply the *'right technique'*
In order to gain His blessing
He was our *'sugar daddy'* and our *'slot machine'*
Dispensing money, blessings – anything really
Whenever we wished

Yet –

All the while
We failed to see how you, Lord

Will topple every idol
We treated your Son, Jesus
As another source of entertainment
We regarded Him
As a figure of love
Willing to give us
All we ever wanted
Your Spirit we regarded
As a source of sensual excitement
Treating Him as our slave
And *'calling Him down'* whenever we wished
He was the *'channel'* we used
To greedily claim our blessings

We even thought that certain politicians
Were hand-picked men of God
Leaders, chosen to save the country
Their political party representing your Kingdom
Yet all they wanted from us were our votes and taxes
We were used and then discarded
They never kept their glibly made promises
And now they've brought us to ruin

How the world laughs at us
"Stupid, dumb Christians!" they call us
Our lust for popularity has backfired
The media views us with scorn
And even the best of people pity us
Shaking their heads and exclaiming
"How did they get into such an awful mess?"

Now reality has caught up with us
And the result is agonizing torment

God –

If you're still there
Please forgive us
For blindly following
The false prophets and false teachers of our age
We hungered for *'signs and wonders'*
<u>But not for you, oh Lord</u>

We mistook our own selfish passions
For the promptings of your Holy Spirit
Through pride, we ignored your correction
And the warning signs you gave –
We ignored any calls to repentance
We glibly dismissed those who told us the truth
As being *'negative and judgemental;'*
'Pharisees!' we called them,
Openly laughing in their faces

Please!!
For the sake of your dear Son
The Lord Jesus Christ
Get us out of this mess
And end this time of wretched desolation

Dear God, forgive us
Remember how your Son
Died for us at Calvary
Recall too His one perfect sacrifice
And His blood poured out
On our behalf

For the sake of Christ
Hold back your wrath
And lighten our chastisements
Free us from our addiction to materialism

Listen to any priestly intercession
He may make for us
Heed any prayers He may offer

Remember too
How He covered all of our sins
Opening the way for us to pray to you
<u>For His sake</u> show us mercy
And grant us the strength to love and to follow you
With a true and whole heart

In this hour of darkness
Disillusionment and despair
Please save us from ruin

<u>And grant us a new beginning</u>
For the glory of your great Name
Take pity on your foolish people
And hear this, our heartfelt prayer, Amen

VULNERABILITY

Oh Lord!

We are in a position of weakness
                          Please strengthen

We are in a position of vulnerability
                          Please protect

We are in a position of terror
                          Please deliver

We are in a position of suffering
                          Please help

We are in a position of strife
                          Please pacify

We are in a position of sickness
                          Please heal

We are in a position of powerlessness
                          Please empower

We are in a position of loss
                          Please redeem

We are in a position of isolation
                          Please come

We are in a position of hunger
                          Please supply

We are in a position of hopelessness
                          Please intervene

We are in a position of homelessness
                                    Please shelter

We are in a position of helplessness
                                    Please restore

We are in a position of exhaustion
                                    Please refresh

We are in a position of destitution
                                    Please provide

We are in a position of despair
                                    Please encourage

We are in a position of dismay
                                    Please comfort

We are in a position of danger
                                    Please protect

We are in a position of confusion
                                    Please guide

We are in a position of anxiety
                                    Please calm

We are in a position of affliction
                                    Please act
Please answer and rescue us
From these great perils
Which torment us, Amen

WHAT HOPE?

What hope is there, oh Lord?
What hope is there?
What can I hope in?
Oh, my soul!
Don't give up, don't give up, don't give up!
Hope in the Lord Jesus Christ
Trust in His goodness
And be confident
That, in due time
He will show you a way through
And deliver you
From your plight, Amen

YOUNG MAN

Young man of twenty what have you seen?

Sights of destruction, death and despair

Why the pale face and the troubled look?

Because I see no hope – only ruin, misery and oblivion

Why the melancholy in your soul?

Because I do not know who I am or what I should do

Why the deep sighs and obvious sorrow?

God is far away, and Jesus has deserted me

Where is your faith?

Gone like a bird, flown from its cage

Young man, do you see any hope?

No, not in this world – only in the next

Where is your love?

Vanished away like a misty vapour

End Notes

Dates following the title show when each piece was first drafted.

Defeated: Sunday, 24th September 2006 at 1.45am. I had been kept awake due to a burning throat infection and violent coughing. It expresses the sense of defeat I was feeling at the time.

Fill: Saturday, 24th April 2010. Written during a time of great personal weariness after praying in languages. New additions were inserted on Friday, 28th May 2010, following a reading of Galatians 5:22-23.

Fog: January 1976. It came to mind whilst waiting at a bus stop in central Newcastle-Upon-Tyne during a cold winter's night. It was amended on Thursday, 15th September 2005 and expresses the sense of desolation I felt when God seemed remote and uncaring

Legacy: Tuesday, 24th August 2004, whilst at Pitlochry Scotland. It expresses a heartfelt wish for the kind of death that will leave behind a good legacy.

Pride: Monday, 13th October 1986 – following a time of worshipping the Lord in spiritual languages. It highlights the need to pray against the sin of pride which, if persisted in, can provoke the Holy Spirit to withdraw His protective blessing.

Relating to Jesus: Sunday, 27th June 2010 whilst at a farmhouse offering Bed and Breakfast accommodation. We were staying at Kilnsea, East Yorkshire, where my wife and I were celebrating our thirty-first Wedding Anniversary.

Relief: Friday, 25th March 2011

Sweep In: Monday, 11th September 2006. Written during the afternoon, seated on a large grey rock after praying in *'spiritual languages'* near the ridge of a certain Moor. It expresses the need to actively seek divine blessing in one's life.

Stand Still: Thursday, 13th June 1990. Written during a prayer retreat, the day after sitting a stiff exam in Management Studies. It expresses the need to rest in God.

They Promised: Monday, 13th October 2008. Much of the phraseology is lifted, word for word, from known false preachers within Pentecostal Christianity. It expresses the mental anguish experienced after personal involvement with Prosperity Teaching.

Vulnerability: Sunday, 28th August 2005. Written in a guesthouse bedroom at Berwick-Upon-Tweed. Its theme is the need to ask for God's help when in great danger and personal weakness. At the time, I had been in fear of my life from a violent drug pusher in my home city.

What Hope? Friday, 6th March 2009, whilst recalling a period of great personal difficulty.

Young Man: Based upon a poem I'd written in April 1976 and re-drafted in December 2016. It expresses how I felt around the age of twenty, during an extremely troubled period in my life.

ACT 4: THE CRISIS

SCENE 1: THE GREAT DELUSION

2 Thessalonians 2:11, *"And for this cause, God shall send them strong delusion, that they should believe a lie."*

A NEW AGE

A 'New Age' is dawning
An Age of counterfeit promises
And Tarot card guidance.
An Age of dark visions
And mystic crystal deceptions

Endless streams of falsehood
Where disharmony and misunderstanding will abound

War will ravage the nations
And hatred will explode across the planet

Minds in bondage
Reason abandoned
Compassion dead

Worship of Self
Worship of Man
Worship of Satan

Yes, a New Age is dawning –
A New 'Dark Age!'

(Is it the Age of the anti-Christ?)

DECEIVER!

I'm a prophet of hope
Whose mission is to help people cope
I give them plenty of rope
To feed off religious dope
I'm a dear friend of the Pope
He really thinks I'm a good bloke
In my work no one is left to mope
I even deliver the odd corny joke

Those old Christians envy my nerve
The New Messiah I gladly serve
He too has plenty of verve
And from his cause I'll <u>not</u> swerve

He saved the world you see
For the special breed of you and me
We couldn't just let things be
Our *'special knowledge'* was the key

I feel so happy about my call
To be His prophet for one and all
With him I gladly stand tall
Not worrying about any fall
As I stride through a temple hall
Those old messiah followers show their gall
But thankfully, they no longer *'set out their stall'*
Because <u>their</u> way (so very long ago) began to pall

There's not a lot more I can tell
The new Messiah has woven his spell
Any revolt he will constantly quell
I feel a great need to yell –
That *"many unbelievers he shall fell
And consign them to the deepest Hell!"*

Hark now, humbly receive his mark
Let him rescue you out of the dark
The choice you face is really very stark
It's most certainly not a lark!

GLOBAL MESSIAH

The world's population has chosen to believe a great delusion
They follow this lie with furious, fanatical fervour
Whilst those few who believe in the truth are persecuted

Hysterical devotion is paid to a global messiah
Who promises an earthly paradise (one that cannot last)
Wearing a demeanour of humility
Whilst attracting all of the glory to himself
His miraculous powers astonish and excite the media
Yet an army of devils form his invisible retinue

Behold!

The world worships a mere man
The sole object of mass adulation
Who promises deliverance from extinction
Songs are written in his praise
And hymns celebrate his alleged deity

Yet he lays only a flawed, floundering foundation
Upon which nothing can stand
He busily makes exciting and enticing promises
Which are broken all too easily

May those who are godly
<u>Not</u> believe in him
May those who are holy
<u>Not</u> give heed to his promises
May those who are righteous
<u>Not</u> quail before his threats

Dear children of light
Don't take fright
Continue to endure
In your faith remain pure
Persevere in the way
That you may see a new day

The Lord honours those
Who remain loyal to Him

In the face of many afflictions
He will show His love
By giving his people strength
To endure a global calamity

Dear children of light
Draw upon God's great might
In His name loyally serve
In your faith never swerve
Believe that Jesus is the way
Trusting he will inaugurate a brand-new day

Let those who are godly
Have confidence in Him
Let those who are holy
Give heed to scriptural promises
Let those who are righteous
Follow their gentle Shepherd

Yes, Jesus is our one flawless, firm foundation
Upon which we stand and rest
Every one of His promises
Will be fulfilled to the very last detail!

Behold!
The world is being laid waste by one man
He is an object of great fear and terror
The human race is on the edge of extinction
Bitter curses replace the songs of praise
And howls of anguish the hymns of celebration

The world's population is paying for this great lie
Bitter recriminations arise from every nation
But those who follow the truth are vindicated
Their heartfelt prayers answered
Many biblical promises are fulfilled
As the curtains of heaven suddenly draw back
And the real messiah arrives in radiant splendour
To install a perfect kingdom
That will bring truth and justice
Let angels and saints loudly rejoice

GNOSTIC CHRIST

Hush my friend,
Pay attention and quietly reflect
When *'it,' 'he'* or *'she'* appears
In mysterious incarnation
A baby, a youth or an old man –
Many are the guises –
An angel, a spirit or a being from outer space
Many are the names of this Christ or Christia
Call them, *'he,' 'she'* or what you will
It really doesn't matter

For: -

I am the Gnostic[47] Christ
A Christ of many forms
A Christ of endless guises

I am the Gnostic Christ
A Christ for all but ...
A Christ for none

I am the Gnostic Christ
A Christ for those with faith
A Christ for those without faith

I am the Gnostic Christ
A Christ of many monasteries
A Christ of many Nunneries

I am the Gnostic Christ
A Christ for Charismatics
A Christ for non-Charismatics

I am the Gnostic Christ
A Christ who is just an ordinary man
A Christ who is a phantom – unable to be touched

---

[47] A *'Gnostic'* was someone initiated into (often) secret, esoteric knowledge. The term is derived from the Greek Word for knowledge, *'Gnosis.'* Gnostic teaching presented a major challenge to the *'Early Church.'*

I am the Gnostic Christ
A *'Zeus'* Christ for Eastern Orthodoxy
A *'Eucharistic'* Christ for Roman Catholicism

I am the Gnostic Christ
A *'Gentleman'* Christ for Anglicanism
A *'Dour, doleful'* Christ for Calvinism

I am the Gnostic Christ
A *'Pacifist'* Christ for Quakerism
A *'Sentimental'* Christ for Liberalism

I am the Gnostic Christ
A *'Witchdoctor'* Christ for Pentecostalism
A *'Rabbinic'* Christ for Messianic Judaism

I am the Gnostic Christ
A *'macho'* Christ for aggressive men
A *'feminised'* Christ for sensitive women

I am the Gnostic Christ
An *'Apollo'* Christ for the Gay community
A *'respectable'* Christ for neo-Conservatives

I am the Gnostic Christ
A *'revolutionary'* Christ, campaigning for justice
A *'mystic'* Christ, present on quiet retreats

I am the Gnostic Christ
A *'militant'* Christ, leading a military crusade
A *'visionary'* Christ, who appears in your dreams

I am the Gnostic Christ
A *'terrorist'* Christ, slaying the enemies of his god
A *'diplomatic'* Christ, promising world peace

I am the Gnostic Christ
A *'cultured'* Christ of the arts
A *'distant'* Christ for the Sciences

I am the Gnostic Christ
A *'seductive'* Christ, who gently beguiles
A *'winsome'* Christ, who sweetly enchants

I am the Gnostic Christ
A *'powerful'* Christ with a *'special anointing'*
A *'loving'* Christ, experience in mystic meditation

I am the Gnostic Christ
A *'laughing'* Christ, scorning your ignorance
A *'tearful'* Christ, pleading for your sympathy

I am the Gnostic Christ
A *'dancing'* Christ, guiding the Cosmos
An *'enlightened'* Christ, bringing us *'true'* philosophy

I am the Gnostic Christ
A Christ of strict morality
A Christ of casual amorality

I am the Gnostic Christ
A Christ who ravishes the heart
A Christ who offends the mind

I am the Gnostic Christ
A Christ who peddles hidden teaching
A Christ who imparts secret knowledge

I am the Gnostic Christ
A Christ flattering human pride
A Christ crushing human opposition

I am the Gnostic Christ
A Christ present in all religions
A Christ offering one true way

I am the Gnostic Christ
A Christ offering a grand *'New Global Order'*
A Christ offering escape from this material world

I am the Gnostic Christ
A Christ inclusive of all races and cultures
A Christ blessing the ruling class alone

I am the Gnostic Christ
A Christ all-inclusive
A Christ almost totally exclusive

I am the Gnostic Christ
A Christ who offers to save without a cross
A Christ who seduces many with lavish promises

I am the Gnostic Christ
A Christ who will woo the masses
A Christ who will rule the nations

I am the Gnostic Christ
A Christ who will display much humility
A Christ who will demand universal worship

I am the Gnostic Christ
A Christ who claims to make you like God
A Christ who, in reality, is anti-Christ

Is he patiently waiting?
Is he biding his time?
Is he poised to reveal himself?
Will he soon appear as a saviour for all of humanity?
Who knows?
But, go my friend
Avoid this false Gnostic Christ (2 Corinthians 11:3-4)
Instead, follow the right Jesus Christ (Galatians 1:6-7)
The One revealed in scripture, (Luke 24:44-48)
The One who died upon the cross (Luke 23:46)
The One who shed His blood to fully atone for your sin
Before rising from the dead (Isaiah 52:13-53:1f)
Indeed, He is the only one who saves (Acts 4:12)
Go to this real Jesus Christ (John 14:6)
Don't equivocate, give Him your allegiance (James 1:5-8)
Ask Him to forgive your sins (Luke 7:47-49)
And to bestow His Holy Spirit (John 20:21-23)
Through Him – receive eternal life (John 3:15)

MAY I NOT SEE

May I not live to see
The anti-Christ rise to power

May I not live to see
The environment destroyed by climate change

May I not live to see
The near destruction of humanity by war, plague and famine

Happy are those who will <u>not</u> live to see these things
For the Lord will have been very merciful toward them
Yet His mercy is present, even amidst the severest of trials
For it is a surprising mercy that sustains and delights us

MISLEADING ADVICE

If it feels good – do it!

If you want something – grab it!

If you want sex – enjoy it!

If you want money – seize it!

If you want success – claim it!

If you want status – take it!

If you want fulfilment – visualise it!

If you want faith – believe it!

If you want to be like God
'Knowing the difference
Between good and evil,' (Genesis 3:5)
Just follow the global messiah
And accept his claims without question

RELAX

Relax, put aside your mind
Subdue any troubling thoughts
Accept what the media says
Be passive, don't think for yourself
Still all of your doubts and *'just go with the flow'*

Now, get ready to follow him
Worship the one who comes
As a *'Prince of Peace'* (Isaiah 9:6)
A *'New Earth'* Messiah (Revelation 21:1)
A deliverer of Humanity
A weaver of many dreams

He will gives us hope
And stills all our fears
His charisma is awesome
His appearance is attractive
His words are soothing
He is like an *'Angel of light'* (2 Corinthians 11:14)
Proclaiming a *'New Gospel'*
Of Global Redemption (Galatians 1:6)

Crowds fall at his feet
Women swoon in his presence
Men are cheered by his company
Possessed by a fervent ecstasy
Many project
Their fantasies onto him
The world will be in his power

Only a troublesome few
Claim he is the devil incarnate
Offering a *'broad way'*
To eternal destruction (Matthew 7:13)
Well, that's their truth
We can ignore it!
For we have with us now
The *'great world teacher'*
Who already fulfils our deepest longings!
Soon, he will have the whole world in his hands!

SOLSTICE TWILIGHT

You sit cross-legged
Amidst a circle of Bronze Age stones
Each standing sentinel-like from a primaeval age
A bronze pentagram
Dangling over your turquoise smock
A mass of curly blond hair
Hangs loosely, lending you
A winsome *'goddess-like'* look
You raise your hands
A blissful smile lighting up your pretty young face
You gaze skyward
Then close your eyes

Clouds chase one another
In windblown procession
On an early mid-summer's evening
Beams of sunlight break through
To dance on the moorland heather
And emblazon a golden sandstone path
But more often, the clouds hide the sun
Behind their spectral, shimmering, silvery wisps

On this Summer Solstice of 2018
A ritual must be performed
The ancestors want it
Their spirits <u>must</u> be appeased!
Sacrifice, mass human sacrifice
Is what they hunger for
But of course, they don't tell <u>you</u> that!
They're consistently pleasant
Whenever they commune with <u>you</u>!
After all, it serves their purpose
To beguile you ever deeper
Into their convoluted mysteries

Hurry!
The *'Ancestral Spirits'* are impatient
With noisy clamour
They demand your worship
Desperate to forget the One

Whose worship they abandoned
Long, long ago
Never mention <u>that</u> Name
Unless it's in mockery or casual anger –
They <u>hate</u> it!

Josticks are lit
Pungent incense wafts into the air
A look of sheer ecstasy
Spreads across your face
Arms soar skywards
As, in a sweet melodic voice,
You chant a hymn –
Composed for Gaia
The Great Mother Goddess
The giver of fertility and bearer of life
You gladly serve her
She is powerful, nurturing and affirming
She is kind, compassionate and healing
You've given your life to her
And you will belong to her forever

It's time now for deep meditation

Arms lowered
Your face turns to the ground
Carefully emptying your mind of all thought
Through deep rhythmic breathing
You are peaceful, you are passive
You are listening

Hark!

They're coming … they're coming!
Carried by the winds of the moor!

The goddess within longs to commune with them
Yes, they speak
They wish to impart some hidden knowledge
A secret ancient wisdom
To aid in your ascension
To another spiritual plane

Something is whispered
About you possessing a *'special healing role'*
In the New World Order
Wherein all of humanity will prosper
In all of its diversity

Oh, you feel love
Nothing but a nurturing, maternal love!
A liquid warmth flows through your body
It's beautiful,
It's wonderful
It's out of this world!
It's coming! It's coming! It's coming!
The message is coming

Images flood in
Of a tall and powerful charismatic figure
In a gigantic stadium,
Full of the sound of melodious hymns
You gasp!
You hear this soft loving voice
<u>You</u> are called to be a healing prophetess
Who will point the way
To he/she/zay – that which is love
All categories will be abolished
To be mystically blended into *'The One!'*

From an adjoining path
And standing near a Trig Point
A bespectacled man
Shouldering his rucksack and walking pole
Watches carefully –
His curiosity kindled.
As a teacher in Religious Studies
He's been *'listening in'* to this lady
Gathering material for a Lecture Course
On Third Millennium, Eclectic, Radical Feminist, Neo-Monistic, Post-Modern Spirituality
He quietly asks himself,
"Do you really know what you've got yourself into?
There's no point in saying anything –
You're too far gone

Best not risk trouble"
Sadly, he shakes his head
And walks away
Down the moorland ridge
Into a Solstice twilight

THE SEEKING

One can seek the truth here
One can seek the truth there
One can seek the truth everywhere

One can seek the truth from Philosophy
One can seek the truth from Religion
One can seek the truth from Science

But all the while it is to be found
In Jesus Christ's words to Nicodemus
"You must be born again,"[48] (John 3:7b)

---

[48] Some translations would suggest *'born from above'* rather than *'born again.'* The wider context of this statement is found in John 3:1-22.

THEY DO NOT SEE

These are a people who rejoice in heresy
Who trifle with God's Word
Who scoff at its warnings
And laugh at its rebukes
Who glibly say, *'It doesn't apply to us'*

These are a people who are smug in their errors
Who wilfully refuse correction
Whose ways are dark and duplicitous
They lure many into eternal darkness
And the raging fires of hell

They do not believe
Because they do not want to believe

They do not see
Because they do not want to see

They do not hear
Because they do not want to hear

They do not perceive
Because they do not want to perceive

They do not discern
Because they do not want to discern

They do not obey
Because they do not want to obey

For, having made an idol of *'self'*
They have been given over
To the lies they wish to believe in

WHY WASTE TIME?

Why seek
To alter the unalterable
Change the unchangeable
Move the immoveable
Reason with the unreasonable?

Is that not the way
To frustration
Fatigue and failure?

Is that not the way
To depression
Despair and defeat?

Instead –
Surely its best to seek the Lord
And yield everything to Him

Is that not the way
To valour
Vindication and victory?

End Notes

Dates following the title show when each piece was first drafted.

A New Age: Sunday, November 4th 1990; concerning the rise of a new *'Dark Age'*

Deceiver: Tuesday, 7th September 2004; concerning the smugness of those who propagate false religion.

Global Messiah: Tuesday, 20th January 2009. It came to mind after watching (on TV) the inauguration of Barack Obama as the forty-fourth president of the United States. However, <u>there was never any intention to suggest that Obama is the anti-Christ</u>; rather that the psycho-sociological dynamics surrounding his inauguration will be replicated on a far greater scale when the anti-Christ <u>does</u> come to power. I view the meteoric rise of Barack Obama as being a *'dress rehearsal'* for this latter event.

Gnostic Christ: Thursday, 20th February 2003. It shows the type of Christ which Mystic Moralism will lead people to worship. It expresses the Chameleon-like qualities of the false Christ – visible in a whole array of guises and stretching throughout history. His highly seductive nature is deliberately emphasised. Performers are welcome to employ the personal pronoun *'He is'* in place of *'I am.'*

May I Not See: Saturday, 1st July 2007. It expresses the yearning to avoid the suffering which will prevail upon the earth shortly before Christ's return.

Misleading Advice: Friday, 30th November 2018. It points out that certain forms of thinking can lure people into serious deception.

Relax: Friday, 30th November 2018. It originally formed a second part to *'Misleading Advice.'* However on Friday, 31st May 2019 the decision was taken to make it into a separate poem.

Solstice Twilight: Monday, 25th June 2018. Loosely based upon an incident seen near the end of a long moorland walk on a previous mid-summer's day (on Thursday, 21st June 2018). At the time, I was wearing a floppy, navy blue sun hat.

The Seeking: Thursday, 19th September 1989 whilst in controversy with a certain Methodist Minister who believed that there were many roads to God. It expresses the view that ultimate truth is only ever to be found in Jesus Christ. John

3:1 reveals that Nicodemus was an influential Jewish religious leader.

They Do Not See: Monday, 13th April 2015. The first two stanzas were added on Friday, 14th October 2016 following a major theological dispute on the Internet over the existence of Hell.

Why Waste Time? Thursday, 23rd April 2015

SCENE 2: THE MARTYRS

Matthew 24:13, *"But he that shall endure unto the end, the same shall be saved."*

ARE YOU WILLING?

Are you willing to love God
With that rational, wholehearted love
Which reaches out to Him?

Are you willing to love God
In a self-sacrificial way –
Placing obedience to His will
Above every other consideration?

Are you willing to love God
With that love which cries out, *'Abba, Father?'*

Are you willing to love God
With that love which declares, *'Jesus Christ is Lord – He came in the flesh to die for my sin?'*

Are you willing to love God
With that love outpoured by His Holy Spirit?

Are you willing to love God
In the face of difficulty, rejection and persecution -
Even from those who call themselves Christians?

Are you willing to love God
At the very moment of death?

Are you willing to love God
By worshipping Him forever
With all of your heart, mind and soul?

Should you be willing, then receive that strength
To follow the God of holy love
Have fellowship with Him
And <u>enjoy</u> His invigorating presence forever!

BRING

Lord
Bring your success
Bring your triumph
Bring your victory
And in the process
Bring my vindication, Amen

ILLUMINATION

Oh Lord
Grant me illumination
And give me the grace
To obey your Word
In all matters –
Even though the cost
May be persecution and death, Amen

LAST THOUGHTS

When I die, oh Lord
Let my last thoughts be of You
And the way you atoned for my many sins at Calvary
Then I will be ready to leave this world to be with You
For whom else is there to believe in?

MY LORD JESUS CHRIST

I stand, swaying on the edge of an abyss
Who will stop me from slipping headfirst?

Unless it be you, my Lord Jesus Christ

My feet slip on an icy slope
Who can hold me up?

Unless it be you, my Lord Jesus Christ

Angry flood waters engulf me
Who can rescue me?

Unless it be you, my Lord Jesus Christ

The ground shudders beneath my feet
Who can preserve my life?

Unless it be you, my Lord Jesus Christ

A large volcano erupts before my eyes
Who can halt its deadly lava flow?

Unless it be you, my Lord Jesus Christ

All my plans have come to nothing
Who will deliver me from failure?

Unless it be you, my Lord Jesus Christ

Necessary provisions have run out
Who can replenish them?

Unless it be you, my Lord Jesus Christ

A terrible disease threatens to consume me
Who can bring about healing?

Unless it be you, my Lord Jesus Christ

Many unseen enemies lay siege to my mind
Who can defeat them?

Unless it be you, my Lord Jesus Christ

The tentacles of death seize hold of me
Who can cut them off?

Unless it be you, my Lord Jesus Christ

My body is slowly decaying
Who can restore it?

Unless it be you, my Lord Jesus Christ

The roaring fires of hell are set to consume me
Who can quench them?

Unless it be you, my Lord Jesus Christ

Endless torment appears to be my fate
Who can save me?

Unless it be you, my Lord Jesus Christ

Now I stand firmly on the rock
Of God's gracious salvation –

Thanks be to <u>you</u>, <u>my</u> Lord Jesus Christ!

PERSECUTION

"A Church aid worker was shot dead yesterday by a man on a motorcycle"

"A Christian church was burnt down last week by a rioting mob."

"The body of a thirteen-year-old girl, the daughter of a Christian Pastor was found lying naked in a field near her village. She had been raped."

"Secret Police disrupted a Christian House Church meeting. All participants were arrested and several severely beaten. The leader is charged with holding illegal meetings."

"Urgent prayers are required for evangelist X whose health is reported to be failing in prison. He has been in solitary confinement for the last two months."

"Mystery death of Christian Pastor during police interrogation raises questions."

"Three female Sunday School teachers have been charged with 'proselytising,' despite an absence of complaints from their neighbours."

"New legislation threatens liberty of churches"

"Christian teacher sacked for criticising the Theory of Evolution in a RE class"

"Human rights lobby threatens to sue inner-city church for alleged intolerance."[49]

Slanderous accusations
Mob violence
Early morning *"knock on the door"*
Is the lot of those
Who remain faithful to Christ
In God-hating countries

---

[49] These are based upon real news bulletins from ministries supporting the persecuted Church.

Fabricated charges
Savage beatings
Cramped punishment cells
Is the lot of those
Who remain faithful to Christ
In God-hating countries

An assassin's bullet
A hangman's noose
A severed throat
Is the lot of those
Who remain faithful to Christ
In God-hating countries

Grieve for those who suffer
Pester the Lord in your prayers
Petition the throne of mercy
Intercede for the helpless
Don't be a bystander
Offer what practical support you can

For one day, their suffering
May well become yours

PLEASE REMEMBER

How I long to see you face to face
And gaze with resurrected eyes
Upon your shining countenance

Ah, Lord Jesus! I long for the day of your return
When you will deliver all of your Saints

I long to be with you
In your New Creation
Where I will see you on your majestic throne

Please remember me on Judgement Day
And take me into your eternal kingdom, Amen

PRIORITIES

What Jesus wants from us
Is not only right doctrine
But a heart responsive to His Spirit
So that we can follow Him joyfully
In His way –
Even though it may lead to death

SEND

Oh, Heavenly father

Please –

Send your Holy Spirit
To give me wisdom in my relationships
And to sustain me amidst great pressure

Send your Holy Spirit
To provide wisdom in decision-making
And to help me resist the allurements of temptation

Send your Holy Spirit
To enable me to endure suffering
And renew me in my unutterable weariness

And finally –

Send your Holy Spirit to make me more like Jesus
When dealing with difficult and stressful people, Amen

THE LEADING

The Lord will guide us
He will show us the right way to go

The Lord will direct us
He will move obstacles from our path

The Lord will lead us
He will educate us in His ways

So, trust in the Father
Submit to the Son
Be led by the Spirit
Into ways that are good

Draw from God's wisdom
Gain strength from <u>His</u> power
Be filled with His grace
And rejoice in His love

THE MARTYR'S PRAYER

Lord, if my death
Is to be a means
Through which millions of people
Come to a real faith
In your Son, the Lord Jesus Christ
Then my death will have been worthwhile

THE SPIRIT CALLS

When
    The Spirit calls you
                To perform a difficult task,
                              <u>Test</u>
        the calling,

<u>Obey</u> the calling,

                And

                        <u>Enjoy</u> the
     calling,

      To the glory

    Of the One
                    Who created
              <u>You</u>
          To love
         And to
      Serve
    Him
   Forever
Amen!

TRUST

Everything breaks apart
No hope of making a new start

Things collapse at a fast pace
Must trust in God's loving grace

All around there's paralysing fear
But to God our Father we're very dear

Boldly trust in Him
Never allow our faith to dim

The world's economy is going slow
A new global system will begin to show

Our society is beginning to fall apart
But from us <u>Jesus will never depart</u>

He's the source of our eternal peace
For us His love will never cease

So, carry on trusting in Him still
Allow your hearts His Spirit to fill

WHEN!

When the whole Church
Turns against Him

Jesus will still be Lord

When duplicitous Church leaders
Ally with a devilish New World Order

Jesus will still be Lord

When careerist Church bureaucrats
Strike Him off their agendas

Jesus will still be Lord

When proud Church theologians
Become champions of falsehood

Jesus will still be Lord

When shallow Church ministers
Mislead gullible congregations

Jesus will still be Lord

When subtle false prophets
Enjoy unbounded popularity

Jesus will still be Lord

When millions of professing believers
Abandon their faith

Jesus will still be Lord

When the powers of deception
Reach a tidal wave crescendo

Jesus will still be Lord

When the human arts and sciences
Are used for thoroughly perverse ends

Jesus will still be Lord

When the turmoil of nations
Breeds chaos and suffering

Jesus will still be Lord

When the people of Israel
Recognise yet another false Messiah

Jesus will still be Lord

When the whole earth
Has joyfully submitted to the anti-Christ

Jesus will still be Lord

When true believers
Become a small, persecuted minority

Jesus will still be Lord

When militant human rebellion
Reaches a peak of mindless hatred

Jesus will still be Lord

When endless numbers perish
In a fiery global destruction

Jesus will still be Lord

When well-armed hordes
Gather against Him

Jesus will <u>show</u> that He is Lord –

To a World and Apostate Church
Allied in war against Him

End Notes

Dates following the title show when each piece was first drafted.
Are You Willing? Wednesday, 8th December 1999, whilst walking to a particular city centre through a thick grey mist. Expressed is the need to accept the challenge to follow the God of holy love. If anyone wishes to respond to this then all they need say is, *"Yes Lord, I am willing to love you with that kind of love, Amen."*
Bring: Wednesday, 29th July 2009 after a frustrating day spent emailing Christian publishers for market research purposes.

Illumination: Monday, 30th November 1981. (last part inserted on Wednesday, 20th May 2009). Written during a time of heavy personal depression, it expresses the need for enlightenment in a period of great darkness.
Last Thoughts: As above
My Lord Jesus Christ: Written during the early hours of Monday, 3rd August 2009, when awake with indigestion caused by overeating the night before!
Persecution: Wednesday, 14th January 2009 and dedicated to all persecuted Christians in the world. In the subsequent ten years, a climate of anti-Christian intolerance has built-up in the Western World – especially inside the United Kingdom.
Please Remember: Friday, 28th January 2011 whilst looking through *'Hymns, Ancient and Modern'*
Priorities: Saturday, 7th January 1984, the final six words being added on Friday, 29th May 2009. It expresses how the Lord would wish for right doctrine and a responsive heart from those who follow Him.
Send: Friday, 16th April 2010, following a period of praying in languages
The Leading: Tuesday, 7th June 2005, whilst walking on a certain Moor. It explores how following God brings peace.
The Martyr's Prayer:, Tuesday, 1st March 2005. Written on a coach trip to Birmingham to attend a business conference. It explores how a Christian's death can fulfil a redemptive purpose.
The Spirit Calls: Saturday, 25th September 2004 whilst on an afternoon coach trip to Manchester. It emphasises how Christians need to respond appropriately to a call from the Holy Spirit to perform a difficult task.
Trust: Saturday, 24th January 2009. Written in response to the economic troubles following the financial crash of September 2008.
When: Sunday, 29th September 2002. It shows that even the worst forms of human rebellion can do nothing to threaten the absolute Lordship of Jesus Christ.

PART B:
ANCIENT LOVE

(Exploring Divine Redemption and the Joy Of
Knowing the Lord Jesus Christ)

INTRODUCTION

Ancient Love shifts emphatically from human rebellion to divine redemption – with the Person and Work of Jesus being wholly central. Highlighted is the way Christ's death upon the cross is the <u>only answer</u> to human sinfulness. Quite deliberately, a contrast is drawn between the ancient hatreds of humanity and the ancient (or eternal) love of God. God's love is open to anyone to receive it, should they (with God's help) choose to believe that the Lord Jesus Christ is their only saviour from sin. Embedded within God's divine redemption is the following causal relationship: -

God's everlasting, passionate love
⇓
A passion to create
⇓
The creation of the universe
⇓
The giving of freewill to both angels and people
⇓
The foundation of Israel
⇓
The redemptive sacrifice of Jesus
⇓
The foundation of the Church
⇓
The restoration of the Jewish people
⇓
The return of Jesus to rescue Humanity from extinction
⇓
The judgement and forcible removal of evil
⇓
The installation of God's perfect kingdom on earth

The emphasis is upon the many wonderful results of salvation (although the awful consequences of rejecting that salvation are not ignored). Hardly surprisingly, there are many worship pieces in **Ancient Love** Each one encourages the believer to participate in the loving fellowship already existing between all three Persons of the Divine Trinity.

ACT 5: THE CROSS

Isaiah 53:10, *"Yet it pleased the LORD to bruise him; he hath put him to grief: when you shall make his soul an offering for sin, he shall see his seed, he shall prolong his days, and the pleasure of the LORD shall prosper in his hand."*

SCENE 1: THE SACRIFICE

BELIEVE ON!

Believe on the Lord Jesus Christ
For He has dwelt with the Father and the Spirit
From all of eternity

Believe on the Lord Jesus Christ
For He has made every particle of Creation
So that all things exist through Him

Believe on the Lord Jesus Christ
For He descended to earth
To become a foetus within Mary's womb

Believe on the Lord Jesus Christ
For He was born of a virgin
Before growing into perfect manhood

Believe on the Lord Jesus Christ
For He was baptised in Jordan's river
To identify with human sin

Believe on the Lord Jesus Christ
For He resisted many temptations
To continue His work as the Son of Man

Believe on the Lord Jesus Christ
For, as teacher, He spoke many wise sayings
And as healer, He performed a myriad of wonders

Believe on the Lord Jesus Christ
For He persevered in following God's will
Even when forsaken by His own disciples

Believe on the Lord Jesus Christ
For He died upon a wooden cross
To accomplish many great things

Believe on the Lord Jesus Christ
For He broke through the bondage of death
And burst forth from the tomb

Believe on the Lord Jesus Christ
For He went up to Heaven
And, from there, sent His Holy Spirit

Believe on the Lord Jesus Christ
For He now works tirelessly
To promote the holiness of believers

Believe on the Lord Jesus Christ
For He receives our worship
And answers our prayers

Believe on the Lord Jesus Christ
For He still blesses us today
By performing many telling wonders

Believe on the Lord Jesus Christ
For He will return as a powerful judge –
A warrior King, toppling strongholds of evil!

Believe on the Lord Jesus Christ
For He will assess our service –
Whether we have been faithful to Him

Believe on the Lord Jesus Christ
For He banishes all who hate Him
Into the endless raging fire of Hell

Believe on the Lord Jesus Christ
For He will receive all things
From His Father, who delights in Him

Believe on the Lord Jesus Christ
For we will stand before Him
Singing His praises for all of eternity

Believe on the Lord Jesus Christ
For there is no better subject to reflect upon
He is worthy of our full attention

Yes, Lord Jesus Christ
Our minds are set on You
Because your greatness is so awesome
Yet mere words, however noble
Can never do You full justice

Truly, You are the inexpressible One
May You be praised and glorified
Throughout all the reaches of eternity
Oh Jesus, we love You

Amen, Amen and Amen!

BLOOD FLOOD

It was long done in the past
Your cleansing from my sin
You shed your holy blood
When on the cross you hung
A spear through your side
To pierce your broken heart
A casual act of deicide
Shown by that sharpened dart
This your work many still oppose –
Just human nature I suppose

FIRST AND FINAL HOPE

Having wandered down many a dark avenue
I can only conclude
That you, Jesus, are my first and final hope
Only in <u>you</u> can I find redemption
And the answer to life's big questions
So, into your hands I commend my spirit
Please blot out my sins and receive me into your kingdom
Have mercy upon me on the Day of Judgement
When the whole of humanity
Will stand before your glorious throne

GIVE GLORY

1.
Give glory to God
For His marvellous attributes

Give glory to God
For His Holy-Love

Give glory to God
For His awe-inspiring Creation

Give glory to God
For His acts in History

Give glory to God
For His wonderful Salvation

Give glory to God
For He <u>is</u> God

2.
Do not give glory to self
For that is to fall into Lucifer's trap

Do not give glory to self
For that is to sin through wretched pride

Do not give glory to self
For that is to provoke the wrath of God

Do not give glory to self
For that will bring about your public disgrace

Do not give glory to self
For that will cause many to despise you

Do not give glory to self
For the end is everlasting destruction

3.
Give glory to Jesus
For He became Man

Give glory to Jesus
For He avoided Satan's snare

Give glory to Jesus
For He is the friend of sinners

Give glory to Jesus
For He does many miraculous works

Give glory to Jesus
For He died to cover over our many sins

Give glory to Jesus
For He arose from the grave

Give glory to Jesus
For He sent His Holy Spirit

Give glory to Jesus
For He will return for His own

Give glory to Jesus
For He shall reign forever

Give glory to Jesus
For He <u>is</u> God –
The only begotten Son of the Father

IF YOU

If you, Jesus
Had not been with me
Disaster would have ensued

If you, Jesus
Had not sustained me
I would have collapsed

If you, Jesus
Had not provided opportunity after opportunity
Everything would have fallen apart

If you, Jesus
Had not sent helpers
My work would have been meaningless

If you, Jesus
Had not removed many obstacles
Then despair would have resulted

Thank you Jesus
For your loving mercy overwhelms me
Without you, I would have been a failure

JOY

Joy
   Joy
      Joy
         Abundant joy
Is what our Father wants to give us, His children

A joy that will endure adversity
Conquer suffering and overcome persecution
A joy founded on His only begotten Son
The Lord Jesus Christ
And His perfect work of sacrifice at Calvary

Joy
   Joy
      Joy
         Abundant joy
Is the gift which God's Spirit freely offers

Oh, you who believe
Do not hesitate
Come to your gracious Father
And receive that eternal joy
Which is in the Lord Jesus Christ
His only begotten Son

LET LOVE

Let love be the foundation of our ministry
Let love be in all we say, think and do
Let love flow through
Unchecked by any deliberate sin
For God's love is mighty and powerful
Yet tender and merciful
But understand this
The love I talk about
Cannot be worked-up by our own efforts
We are not able to produce such a love
By sheer willpower alone
No, my friend, it is a love
Which is freely given
A love which God Himself bestows

Follow Jesus and obey Him as your Lord
Yield all your sins to Him
(His Spirit will point them out to you)
Then you will become full-grown in love
It will flow through you naturally
Without it being forced on your part
Grow in this love
Submit to this love
Rejoice in this love
Then your ministry will grow
And help to change people's lives

By building upon the Father's love
(Shown through the death of His Son)
You will be building a sure foundation

LOVE NOT

Love not your status
As a *Teacher-Preacher*[50]
Do not exalt yourself
Above the humble believer
Or cultivate a superficial spirituality
Which God hates
To do so commits the sin
Of the Scribes and Pharisees
Whom Jesus condemned in public

Rather
<u>Let the responsibilities of ministry</u>
<u>Teach you humility</u>
Learn to show compassion
In the small things
As well as the larger issues
Show tolerance toward those
Who are slow in understanding
Be careful to sympathise with the weak

Recall, with heartfelt gratitude
What Jesus did for you
Through His sacrificial death
Notice how, despite His full Deity
He humbled Himself
To die horribly for <u>you</u>
On the cross of torture
Take this to heart
So you will not fall into vanity

Remember,
<u>All true ministry</u>
<u>Operates in a school of humility</u>
And <u>not</u> in pride

---

[50] Readers may wish to substitute their own ministry in place of *'Teacher-Preacher.'*

OH JESUS!

Oh Jesus! How incredible you are
Even when viewed from afar
In merciful grace you humbly took
A human frame, of no distinguished look

You did not come as a mighty king
Humility being very much your thing
Mortal frailty you knew only too well
But you resisted the powers of hell

You grew as a humble Jewish man
Living under the Mosaic ban
You faced the struggles of a peasant life
And saw the cruelty of civil strife

Baptismal waters, important to meekly accept
But no sin in you could anyone detect
An offer of worldly power you refused
Satan's poisoned promises you defused

With great patience you delivered, healed and taught
Prompting in your audience much needed thought
You exposed the errors of your day
Refusing to allow them any last say

By wicked men you were tortured and slain
Nailed to a cross – you felt agonizing pain
Yet to the very last hour your love blazed out
Your life closed with a loud defiant shout!

Cruel powers of Hell you managed to disarm
To ensure they didn't do us any harm
In great might you rose from the dead
Showing Creation you were its one true Head

To frail, foolish followers you kindly sent
Your Holy Spirit who came in fiery descent
Good News the apostles began to proclaim
Now nothing would ever remain the same

Your gospel then spread throughout the earth
Ending a cruel spiritual dearth
Mighty Empires – they grew and fell away
But your message is still around today

In awesome majesty you shall return
Honouring those of faith who remain firm
In eternal splendour you will reign
Having, at the last, put an end to all pain

SIN BIN

Like a nest of greedy rats
Are my many sins

Like a dish of plague bacilli
Are my many iniquities

Like a tumour of deadly cancerous cells
Are my many faults

Who can save me from myself?

Like a raging firestorm
Are my many selfish passions

Like an uncontrolled hurricane
Are my many lustful desires

Like an exploding volcano
Are my many vengeful hatreds

Who can save me from myself?

Like a swirling whirlpool
Are my many trembling, timid fears

Like a roaring waterfall
Are my many restless, changeable ambitions

Like a polluted river
Are my many empty-headed boasts

Who can save me from myself?

Like a deeply hidden cavern
Are my many dark motivations

Like a long-forgotten grave
Are my many buried ideals

Like a blocked-up tunnel
Are my many thwarted hopes

Who can save me from myself?

Like a massive crashing tidal wave
Are my many fallen yearnings

Like an evaporating steamy jungle mist
Are my many useless ideas

Like a barren parched desert
Are my many attempts to do good

Who can save me from myself?

Like thin wispy air currents
Are my kindly aspirations

Like a shimmering mirage
Are my religious ways

Like a useless nothingness
Are my attempts to find God

Who can save me from myself?

Only Jesus can –
Through his cleansing blood
Shed upon a wooden cross, Amen

THE WAY

He is *'the way, the truth and the life'*
The only name in Heaven and on Earth
Whereby we can be saved –
The only means whereby
We may receive forgiveness of sin
And enjoy a personal relationship with God

So –

Repent of all your selfish ways
Turn to Jesus Christ
Believe Him to be your Saviour
Obey Him as your Lord
Worship Him as your God
For in Jesus – our King
A perfect holy-love exists

It is He who rescues us from sin
Delivers us from evil and brings us to God
So that we can know Him as Father
Rather than as condemning Judge

So, my friend, be filled with
His Spirit
His wisdom
His power
Receive the fullness of His grace
Turn from the futility of your own ways

Enjoy the tender goodness of God
Enjoy the good things in His Creation
Enjoy the many blessings He kindly bestows
Grow in His ways –
In direct contrast to the ways of this world

Allow Him to change your life –
By replacing bad with good attitudes
Permit His Spirit to break all bad habits
When He chooses to do so
Then, with bold sensitivity

Testify to others
That Jesus is *'the way, the truth and the life'*
The <u>only</u> source of salvation
Who can bring us into an eternal relationship
With God, our gracious Father

THIS IS THE DEATH

This is the death that saved a sin-stricken world
And gave many blessings to all

This is the death that fulfilled scriptural promises
And showed us God, honouring his Holy Word

This is the death that permitted Creation's existence
And set limits to God's judgement upon the earth

This is the death that quenched God's vengeful wrath
And released us from a condemning Law

This is the death that revealed a Father's tender love
And *'covered over'* our dreadful sins

This is the death that made Jesus our friend
And filled us with His gracious Spirit

This is the death that smashed Satan's schemes
And rescued us from a raging, boiling Hell

This is the death that delivered us from evil's grasp
And caused demons to flee, screeching in terror

This is the death that humbled self-righteousness
And brought to nothing human pride

This is the death that justified us before a Holy God
And made us His adopted children

This is the death that restrained our sinful nature
And enabled us to become more like Jesus

This is the death that inspired a range of good works
And prompted us to share His Gospel

This is the death that engendered great, musical wonders
And led to creative works of dramatic art

This is the death that stirred these joyful words
And filled my heart with a fulsome hope

This is the death to be celebrated for all of eternity

WAVE UPON WAVE

Wave upon wave of anger
Wave upon wave of hatred
Wave upon wave of outrage
Is thundering against our shores
Eroding the very foundation
Of our once great Civilization –
Hatred rules OK!

All I can see in our political discourse
Is a bubbling, boiling, burning fury
Seething across the Social Media
A scalding, searing and spitting lava flow
Of distinctive, destructive rhetoric

Truly, there is …

Little light
Little truth
Little integrity
Ideologues are governed
By unquiet passions
That stir-up no end of strife
Whilst the rest of the people
Are addicted to empty pleasures
That dull the mind

Are we staggering down the road to Armageddon?
A raucous party of quarrelling drunks
Out on a Saturday night binge?

Is the great *'world-deceiver'*
Poised to spring from his hidden place
To seduce the world's population?
Will he use technology to cement his tyranny
And destroy the lives of billions?
Is this the age of the anti-Christ?

Who knows?

But I do know that
We can be saved – through faith
In the perfect Blood Sacrifice of Jesus Christ
Which procured the forgiveness of our sins
He appeased God's justified wrath
Against our many iniquities

Only He can redeem!
Only He can make whole!
Only He can give eternal life!
In Him is freedom from delusion
His Spirit gives true enlightenment

So ...

Trust in Jesus
Commend your ways to Him
Ask Him to be your Saviour and Lord
Invite Him into your life
Let His Spirit guide you
Follow His will – once it has been discerned
Place no trust in any self-proclaimed world messiah
For only in Jesus is there hope
He alone can bring true love and fulfilment

End Notes

Dates following the title show when a piece was first drafted
Believe On! Wednesday, 5th July 1989 at the beginning of a prayer retreat. The opening words of each verse *"Focus Upon Jesus,"* being changed to the more biblical *"Believe upon the Lord Jesus Christ"* during the final revision in November 2002, (Acts 16:31).It expresses the importance of giving Jesus Christ the full attention of our minds.
Blood Flood: Wednesday, 4th August 2004 when beginning a prayer retreat, accompanied by fasting. Its theme is the continuing opposition the human race displays toward the sacrificial work of Jesus Christ upon the cross
First and Final Hope: Tuesday, 30th October 2012
Give Glory: Tuesday, 6th January 2009 during a New Year's retreat. It expresses the need to give glory to God alone – when severely tempted to indulge in the sin of self-glorification!
If You: Friday, 29th June 1990 – the day after I'd received news of passing some very stiff postgraduate exams (The Diploma in Management Studies). It expresses the personal relief felt due to divine deliverance. At the time I was so exhausted by the pressures of this course that I'd been suffering from anxiety attacks.
Joy: Monday, 15th December 1986. It expresses the way Christ wants us to share in His joy
Let Love: Sunday, 10th November 1985, expressing the need to consciously yield to divine love.
Love Not: Tuesday, 5th May 2009.
Oh Jesus: Saturday, 22nd January 2011 whilst looking at Hymn 187 in *'Hymns, Ancient and Modern.'* The aim was to experiment with new forms of poetry
Sin Bin: Saturday, 18th September 2004. It expresses how an awareness of sin can point people to the Lord Jesus Christ
The Way: Wednesday, 14th January 2009
This is the Death: Tuesday, 10th August 2004. It expresses the multi-faceted nature of Christ's death and how it can encourage poetical celebration.
Wave upon Wave: Monday, 14th May 2018

SCENE 2: THE FORGIVEN

Psalm 32:1, *"Blessed is he whose transgression is forgiven, whose sin is covered."*

AWESOME GRACE

I once was lost in *'sin and nature's night'* [51]
Into many a trap and snare I fell
My whole life was consumed by a relentless blight
I often felt as if I were eye-deep in Hell
But incredibly, I found mercy in your sight

You, oh Lord, saved me
You, oh Lord, redeemed me
You, oh Lord, delivered me
Through your death upon the cross

I found your gospel to be no con
Your Word and Spirit urged me on
Wretched I may once have been
But now I can write on a joyful theme
To you I can thankfully fly
As your Word contains no lie

You, oh Lord, saved me
You, oh Lord, redeemed me
You, oh Lord, delivered me
Through the blood you shed on the cross

Thank you Jesus, for your awesome grace
Help me to follow you at a measured pace
And in eternity I will see you face-to-face

---

[51] A phrase from the Charles Wesley Hymn *'And Can It Be?'*

DEAR JESUS!

Dear Jesus!
Move in with
Your love
Your holiness
Your compassion
Your power
Your grace
Your justice
And please …
Get me out of the mess I'm in! Amen

CONFIDENCE

Oh death, you have the power to take my life
But you do not have the power to send me to Hell
For I have been redeemed by the blood of Jesus Christ

FIRMLY MOORED

In you, oh Lord
My faith is moored
In silence I rest
In you I am blest

Behold, you come and speak
As your will I earnestly seek
Your Spirit refreshes my soul
And gives me a definite, clear goal

Your gentle presence resides in my heart
Kindly offering a completely new start
Oh Father, I love it when you are near
For in you I find there's *'nowt'* to fear!

FOR MY SIN

On your bread and wine I feed
For my sin you once did bleed
In that wonderful great deed

Let me take heed
As you give a lead
To meet my great need

Your blood still does plead
So I can grow like a seed
Please pluck out every sinful weed

GRACE AND MERCY

Ah! How awesome is your mercy, oh Lord

Can we fathom it?
Can we understand it?
Can we grasp its ways?

Through it you remove our sins
As far as the East is from the West (Psalm 103:12)

Can we respond to all of your kindness?
Can we honour all of your love?
Can we appreciate all of your forgiveness?

Truly, the immensity of your love fills us
With a speechless awe

Through Christ's sacrifice you display it
Through Christ's death you reveal it
Through Christ's offering you show it

Christ gave me access to you, despite my habitual iniquities
Now the challenge is to show grace and mercy to others
By relying upon your grace alone

GRATITUDE

How thankful I am
That you do not treat me
As my sins deserve

How relieved I am
That you have forgiven
All of my many faults

How overwhelmed I am
By the greatness of your mercy
So freely and generously given

How grateful I am
That you spared me your wrath
And that you treat me like a son

How enthralled I am
At the tender goodness
You regularly show me

How awed I am
By the redemption you wrought
Through your blood sacrifice at Calvary

Without it, I and many others
Would deservedly face an eternal exile
From your gracious presence

OPEN

Lord Jesus Christ, open the eyes and ears
Of both the Jewish and Gentile Worlds
To your precious Gospel
So that millions can receive
The salvation you purchased so dearly
For them at Calvary, Amen

PRIORITY

The most important
Thing in life
Is to find God
And from then on
To follow Him
Every step of the way
Until such time
As He is pleased
To take you to Himself

SOAKING

I'm soaking in the Spirit of God
He causes many prayers to flow from my lips
In heavenly languages I sing praises
To the most-high King
A brooding presence fills me with strength
As words of scripture leap from the page
Hard decisions I'm free to make
As a peaceful clarity of mind takes hold
Sin starts to burn away
When, in a holy stillness I wait
Enjoying an intelligent communion with Jesus
Yes, it's good being filled with the Spirit of God

THANKSGIVING

Thank you God
For your great salvation
For your great redemption
For your great deliverance
Thank you God for being God –
The God of Holy-Love

THE POOR MAN

Do not despise the poor man
Nor speak with undue sharpness to the beggar
Know that you too
Are poor in God's sight
Your own sins leaving you feeling
Like an impoverished wanderer inside

Remember too that Jesus
Is the friend of sinners and outcasts
He too is: -
A refuge for those despised by society
A protector of the downtrodden
A shelter for the homeless

Listen and understand –
It is only by divine grace
That you have been so enriched
Even when you think it best
To refuse a vagrant any money
(Lest he destroys himself with drink)
Speak to him kindly
And show him as much courtesy
As you would to Jesus, your saviour

Show mercy because you have been shown mercy
Display kindness because the Lord is kind
Listen to His rebuke
So that you will learn to hear His voice
And see His ways
In everyday incidents
Apply all of the things His Holy Spirit teaches
So that you will be able to pass on
All of the resources you've been given

Above all – make love your aim
Permit the love of Jesus
To flow straight through you

End Notes

Dates following the title show when each piece was first drafted.
Awesome Grace: Saturday, 14th May 2011. Strongly emphasised is the theme of sin and redemption. (It came to mind after hearing the 1960's pop group *The Animals'* singing the traditional American folk song *'House of the Rising Sun'* on *'YouTube.'*)
Dear Jesus: Thursday, 16th September 2004. It expresses the need to invoke Christ's help when in a crisis.
Confidence: Saturday, 22nd January 2011
Firmly Moored: Saturday, 22nd January 2011 whilst on private retreat. The colloquial *'nowt'* reflected my sense of simple joy and reverent intimacy with the Lord.
For my Sin: Tuesday, 10th August 2004. It expresses the believer's total dependence upon Christ's sacrificial blood to promote spiritual growth.
Grace and Mercy: Saturday, 30th October 2010
Gratitude: Wednesday, 20th October 2010
Open: Tuesday, 14th September 2004. It expresses the need to use prayer as a means of spreading the Gospel.
Priority: Tuesday, 28th June 1983. It expresses God's overwhelming importance in our lives.
The Poor Man: Thursday, 12th December 1985 – a few days after I'd harshly dismissed a vagrant who'd stopped me to ask for money outside a major shopping centre. I later helped the poor man in question by referring him to a particular local government department which I thought would benefit him. In appearance, he was a little man with an unshaven face and old-fashioned National Health Spectacles. Sometimes, he wore a battered black hat. I saw him on a number of occasions.
Soaking: Tuesday, 8th September 2009 whilst reflecting upon a monastic retreat I'd enjoyed the previous weekend
Thanksgiving: Saturday, 6th November 2010.

ACT 6: THE CALLING

SCENE 1: THE COMMISSIONING

Jeremiah 1:5a, *"Before I formed you in the belly I knew you; and before you came forth out of the womb, I sanctified you."*

CARRY ON

Carry on
Don't give up
Persevere
And persist in the cause
Which God
Has shown you

The battle is hard
But Jesus is with you
To give you
An incomparable victory
Over your enemies

Carry on
Don't give up
Or waiver
In your determination
Avoid being double-minded
Brace yourself
For action
And listen carefully

God will give you
A will of iron
To accomplish your mission
(To witness to Christ's truth)
Your face
Will be set like concrete
Hard as flint –
You shall continue undaunted
In your purpose

Ignore those who say
'He goes his own way
He will not work with other people
He refuses to be under any authority'
For: -
Jesus is your way
Jesus is your work
Jesus is your authority
And in Him
The *'Word made flesh'*
You will find peace

CASCADE

Words cascade like bubbling water from my heart
Images flash and dart like forked lightening in my mind
Ideas swirl like a mighty hurricane through my brain
My whole being is lit up by a pulsating spiritual energy
That locks my will into a single resolute course

Deliberately and methodically
I prepare to confront
An *'infernal'* intelligence
By hurtling a barrage of truth-telling books
Into an indifferent and unsuspecting world…
 "Sorry m'love,' Ah din't 'ear yer shout
"TEA'S READY!"
Ah'll come soon,
Honest ah will
Don't yell
'IT'S GETTING COLD!'
Ah'm busy on the Computer
Ah'll come soon"

When eventually I did come downstairs
And enter the kitchen
My tea was cold!

COMMISSIONED!

You have filled me
With your Spirit of grace
A supernatural calm
Fills my heart
I see clearly
The right way to go

You are the excellent One
You are the glorious One
You are the Lord most high

You have equipped me
For a very hard task
The sword of truth
Has been sharpened
And is now ready to confront
A spiteful, backslidden people

You are the excellent One
You are the glorious One
You are the Lord most high

You have raised me from nothing
To be a scourge
To those grown accustomed
To despising your Word
They shall be forced to face the truth
Of your Holy wrath

You are the excellent One
You are the glorious One
You are the Lord most high

You have commissioned me
To fulfill an unusual call
By your power alone
It can be accomplished
My face has become like flint
A firm purpose grips my heart

You are the excellent One
You are the glorious One
You are the Lord most high

You have encouraged me
To directly challenge
The complacency of those who are smug
I have been given a will of titanium steel
All hesitation has gone
My conscience enjoys a quiet peace

You are the excellent One
You are the glorious One
You are the Lord most high

You planned this call
Long before I was born
You conceived this path
From eternal ages past
And set me on a collision course
With an apostate Church

You are the excellent One
You are the glorious One
You are the Lord most high

You amaze me with your works
The wisdom you display
Is beyond compare
Praise be to you Father, Son and Spirit
Let me extol you
For the greatness of your love

You are the excellent One
You are the glorious One
You are the Lord most high –
My only Lord!

DISCOURSE

Discourse, discourse, discourse
On the Atonement
Expound its mysteries to the people
To whom the Lord leads you

Delve deep into the scriptures
Base all you say upon His Word
Allow Holy Writ to determine the content of your teaching
Go to them, go to them
Go to those who doubt and say: -
"What Jesus did *is the very foundation of your life.*"

Exhort them <u>not</u> to be in two minds
Warn them <u>not</u> to stay on the fringes of Christ's kingdom
Invite them to come in and know His fullness
Invite the young in faith to whom God leads you
Invite them by using the methods He shows you

FAITH

This is the faith
We are to cleave to
A faith which has its origins in eternity
A faith founded upon Jesus Christ as Lord and Saviour
A faith given by the Holy Spirit

Believe, without doubt
That Jesus is indeed the true God
Who took on the limitations of humanity
Without losing any of the attributes of His Deity
Who became a clump of cells
In a Virgin's womb
And then grew up to serve many

He died upon the cross
Shedding His life-giving blood
To be a sacrifice for sin
To appease divine wrath
And to be a proof of divine love

Acknowledge too
That He gave His righteousness
In exchange for your sin
Respond in repentance and faith
Place yourself in His care

Let His Spirit give you wisdom
To understand all of these things
Publicly witness that it is Jesus Christ's atonement
Which forms the basis of your life

Place no faith in your own efforts
But rather have confidence
In the work Jesus did at Calvary

It is in that and that <u>alone</u>
Wherein lies your salvation
Accept God's free gift of forgiveness
Which <u>the cross alone provides</u>

Allow this forgiveness
To create a new beginning in your life
And to form a mainspring for every good deed

Hold no doubt as to its sufficiency
For Christ's work of atonement
Is complete and needs <u>no</u> repetition

FEAR NOT

Fear not this present darkness
Do not be anxious
About the perplexity you suffer
Avoid worrying over decisions
God is calling you to make
For, although you don't see Him
He is with you
To uphold and strengthen you
To open up the path
Along which you should travel

In your very weakness <u>God is present</u>
Working in ways
Which you could not
<u>Even begin</u> to imagine
Already, His Holy Spirit
Is helping you to pray
He will guide you into those intercessions
Which should be made

Hold onto the faith
He has given you
Hold onto that faith
So that you will be able to receive
Those blessings you so strongly desire

FOLLOW

Follow the inspiration that comes from on High
Let it grow and develop
Like an embryo in the womb

Follow the inspiration that is God's gift to you
Let it gently fill your heart
Stir your emotions and enlighten your mind

Follow the inspiration that is Heaven's true calling
Let it carve out a new path in your life
And lead you away from waterless places

Follow the inspiration that points in the right direction
Let it produce many creative works
That will challenge the evils of our time

GLAD SURRENDER

Abba Father
Through your Son the Lord Jesus Christ
And under the direction of your Holy Spirit

I gladly surrender to you
My hidden *'spiritual'* self
With its
Meditations
Worship
Prayers
Intercessions
And sweet encounters with you

Burn out any sin
And fill me
With your good Holy Spirit

I gladly surrender to you
My inner *'psychological'* self
With its
Drives
Passions
Emotions
Thoughts
And decision-making abilities

Burn out any sin
And fill me
With your good Holy Spirit

I gladly surrender to you
My outer *'physical'* self
With its
Head
Torso
Limbs
Appendages
And unique individual characteristics

Burn out any sin
And fill me
With your good Holy Spirit

I gladly surrender to you
My *'private-personal'* life
With its
Joys
Sorrows
Friendships
Chores
And many petty vexations

Burn out any sin
And fill me
With your good Holy Spirit

I gladly surrender to you
My *'public worldly'* life
With its
Activities
Demands
Opportunities
Threats
And abundance of contacts

Burn out any sin
And fill me
With your good Holy Spirit

I gladly surrender to you
My *'eternal heavenly'* life
With its
Judgements
Perfections
Relationships
Love
And ceaseless fellowship with you

Burn out any sin
And fill me
With your good Holy Spirit

Thus, oh Lord
By your grace
I surrender everything to you
Everything I am
And everything I ever will be

Burn out any sin
And fill me
With your good Holy Spirit
Now and forever

GRANDSON

In my arms I cradle my baby grandson
Listening to his content cooing
I pause to think of the world he'll grow up in
Then – with firm resolution I decide
'It's time to make a stand
And speak out about what's happening in our society'

"For your sake, I will not remain quiet
For your sake, I will not remain passive
For your sake, I will not remain silent
I will speak out about the evils in our time
Saying what needs to be said

In later life may you appreciate the stand your Grandfather took"

LET ME RUN

Let me run
Let me flee
Let me escape
Into your presence, oh Lord
Where, united in love
I can be in you
And you in me
For all eternity, Amen

MOTIVE

Let love of truth
Be the motive of my studies
For in loving the truth
I also love Jesus
Who is the Truth

Pursue my research diligently
Steep it in prayer
Draw encouragement from sermons
Given in my local Christian Community
Build upon the foundation of scripture
Then I will not go astray

Do not be like those theologians
Who seek only fame
Do not be like those
Who seek to escape personal problems
Through the avenue of study
Whilst viewing their daily employment
As some dry chore

By God's grace
I will endeavour to ensure that
Having the right motives
God will grant me success

SENT

The Lord sent me to confront
A rebellious people
A people who are without: -
Comprehension
Discernment
Knowledge
Or understanding
Of the Holy-One of Israel

The Lord sent me to confront
A rebellious people who are full of: -

Heresy
Pride
Stubbornness
And wilfulness
Toward the Awesome Creator who made them

The Lord sent me to confront
A rebellious people
A people who love to indulge in: -
Clamorous argument
Endless debate
Sarcastic sneers
False teaching
About the Almighty King who is judging them

SERVE

Go out! Go out!
Feed the hungry
Care for the sick
Visit those in prison
And champion the rights of the deprived
Understand this –
God does not send His Spirit
For you to stay in insular *'Holy Huddles'*
Nor does He bless you with His gifts
For you to keep them all to yourselves
Rather, He bestows these gifts upon you
So that you can be of practical use
Within this World
They were given to aid evangelism
With deeds of love
Abandon the silly notion
Which leads you to say,
'We are in the forefront of God's purposes
So we can despise and ignore Christians
From other traditions'

Doing this would cause you to
Move further away from His plans
And you will have inflicted much grief
Upon the Person of His Spirit

THE CHARGER

God is my charger and warhorse
God is my stirrups and spur
God is my saddle and reins
God is my sword and shield
God is my helmet and breastplate

Get ready to go <u>now</u>

And
CHARGE!

Enter
Enemy strongholds

Attack
Destructive influences

Thwart
Deceptive stratagems

For the Lord is with me
To give a stunning victory
The struggle will be long and hard
But I will triumph mightily
Because of His grace

THROUGH

Through His Holy Spirit
Jesus calls me
Jesus convicts me
Jesus saves me

Giving me much power
And the desire
To serve you God, my Father

Through His Holy Spirit
Jesus consecrates me
Jesus enlightens me
Jesus heals me

Giving me a gentle wisdom
And the discernment
To serve you God my Father

Through His Holy Spirit
Jesus captivates me
Jesus fills me
Jesus touches me

Giving me the compassionate love
And the determination
To serve you God my Father

Through His Holy Spirit
Jesus consumes me
Jesus matures me
Jesus purifies me

Giving me a reverence for God's word
And the doxology
To praise you God my Father

WHY ME?

Why me, oh Lord?

Are you really calling me to the task of confronting the Anglican Church?

Why me, oh Lord?

Couldn't you send someone else to do this unrewarding work?

Why me, oh Lord?

Aren't others better qualified than I to do this awful job?

Why me, oh Lord?

Nothing good will come of it!

Why me, oh Lord?

No one will heed my warnings!

Why me, oh Lord?

These are a people whose leaders I despise!

Why me, oh Lord?

Let these leaders wallow in their own corruption!

Why me, oh Lord?

It's ridiculous, absurd, stupid and impossible!

Why me, oh Lord?

Trouble and ruin will be my only reward!

Why me, oh Lord?

What use is there in doing this?

Why me, oh Lord?

Please don't press me with your Spirit!

Why me, oh Lord?

By a multitude of circumstances
You confirm this call!

But why me, oh Lord?
Zealously you pursue me
To accomplish this awful task
Of confronting a decadent Church –
Which has long-since grown deaf
To the voice of your Spirit

End Notes

Dates following the title show when each piece was first drafted.

Carry On: Saturday, 8th July 1989, at a time when I was enduring hostile criticism from a local church leadership. They would subsequently endorse the error of the Kansas City Prophets (KCP). (A group of spiritualists associated with the American *'healing evangelist,'* John Wimber.) The KCP brought many pagan and New Age influences into the Church. Influenced by their prophecies John Wimber (1934-1997) made a public fool of himself by predicting a mighty revival for Britain which would breakout in October 1990. This never materialized. Conversely, the 1990s saw a further deterioration in the condition of the British Churches (Deuteronomy 18:22). I saw first-hand some of the confusion and hurt to have arisen from this fiasco.

Cascade: Saturday, 24th March 2007, just before I released my first book; *The 52 Attributes of God'* for publication. It conveys the excitement felt during a period of intense creativity.

Commissioned: Monday, 22nd September 2003. It conveys the sense of wonder when called by God to carry out a humanly impossible task. (This centered upon tackling the serious errors present within the Church of England.)

Discourse: Wednesday, 17th February 1988. It prompted me to give my first theological workshop on Saturday, 9th April 1988. It was entitled *The Pivot of Faith,'* and explored our Lord's atonement in great depth. (The material was further expanded and incorporated into my book *The 'Leeds Liturgy'* in a section entitled, *'A Shorter Celebration of Christ's Work upon the Cross.'*)

Faith: Sunday, 28th February 1988, when preparing for *The Pivot of Faith'* conference. It explored the total sufficiency of Christ's work upon the cross.

Fear Not: Wednesday, 29th August 1990, during a retreat. It expresses the importance of holding onto one's faith in a time of great personal darkness.

Follow: Wednesday, 17th January 2012. Written during a certain cultural event, at a time of great personal disappointment. These events all took place following a breakdown in my relationship with the mainstream Churches.

Glad Surrender: Saturday, 26th February 2005. Written on a coach journey from Manchester.

Grandson: Friday, 22nd January 2010.

Let Me Run: Thursday, 10th September 2009. Written whilst on a private prayer retreat.

Motive: Thursday, 23rd June 1988. Written on our ninth wedding anniversary and three months before launching into teaching various Christian groups. By the end of 1989, considerable success had been gained in the church teaching area. It began with a bible teaching ministry that would impact upon many people over the next decade.

Sent: Friday, 18th June 2004, on the same day this piece was placed on the internet and triggered an acrimonious discussion concerning the poetry of (the then Archbishop of Canterbury) Rowan Williams. *'Sent'* was expressed as a challenge to myself to confront a rebellious people who have no interest in knowing the truth. My controversial involvement in the Anglican area would last from June 2004 until August 2008. After that date I never returned to the Anglican Sector; I'd washed my hands of it.

Serve: Friday, 12th December 1986. This poem was sent (early the following year) to a Christian group who belonged to what was then known as *The Restoration Movement.'* (In 1994, it was to embrace the deception of the Toronto Blessing and I saw overt demonic activity in one of its

meetings.) This poem stresses that God wants us to use His gifts to serve others and <u>not</u> to puff-up our own sense of self-worth.
The Charger: Tuesday, 6th February 1986. It expresses faith in God's ability to give victory in spiritual warfare.
Through: Saturday, 25th September 2004. It looks at how Jesus works (through His Holy Spirit) to bless and enable the believer to serve God, their Heavenly Father.
Why Me? Sunday, 16th February 2003, whilst wrestling with a call to confront certain errors within the Church of England.

SCENE 2: THE TESTIMONY

Revelation 19:10, *"I fell at his feet to worship him. And he said unto me, See thou do it not: I am thy fellow servant, and of thy brethren that have the testimony of Jesus: worship God: for the testimony of Jesus is the spirit of prophecy."*

A CRY FOR DELIVERANCE

"In the name of Jesus Christ, stop!"

The presence stopped about a couple of yards to the right of me and remained floating in front of a shelf full of books.[52] Despite my utter panic I dimly discerned that this spirit was far more terrified of Jesus than I was of it. Suddenly, I felt an enormous pressure forcing down my right shoulder and causing that half of my body to shake violently. It was like having an epileptic fit[53] except that my mind remained crystal clear. This spirit seemed to want to enter inside me. Thankfully, it wasn't able to because the Holy Spirit was already there, deep inside my heart and mind. As this pressure gradually increased I cried out: -

---

[52] One of which (appropriately) was William Sargant's *'Battle for the Mind'*
[53] I had <u>never</u> previously (except for this one moment) experienced <u>any</u> kind of fit

"I call upon you,
Yes you, the Highest God
Who has rescued me from many difficult situations?[54]
Save me from this evil
Honour your word of scripture[55]
And in this hour of darkness
Outpour your Spirit
And double,
        Treble,
                Quadruple
The number of angels
Sent to protect me!
Amen."

At this point four Christians (who had been praying in an upstairs lounge) entered the room and the warden (a Methodist lay preacher) ordered the spirit to depart in the name of Jesus. My prayer for deliverance had been answered. That night I slept for eleven hours – both emotionally and mentally exhausted.

---

[54] I then proceeded to mention some of the difficult situations which the Lord had seen me through – one of which was an encounter with a white witch and heroin addict who'd spoken in tongues. This had happened whilst undertaking social work amongst drug addicts in Notting Hill, London during the previous August (1976).

[55] The previous week (whilst in Newcastle-Upon-Tyne) I had been reading (from the Jerusalem Bible) Romans 10:13 which (itself quoting from Joel 3:5) contained a marvellous promise of salvation. During the warm and sunny afternoon of September 5th an Asian Christian girl had shared with me the same passage and told me how the Lord had delivered her from an evil influence.

BIT-BY-BIT

Bit-by-bit
Little-by-little
Moment-by-moment
It's happening

Phase-by-phase
Stage-by-stage
Step-by-step
It's happening

What's happening?

The gradual up-building
Of God's kingdom
In my life

CLOUD WATCHING

On a neatly cut grass slope I lie
Looking upward to the sky
Sleepily watching clouds drifting by

In slow, windblown procession
They follow in orderly progression
Whilst I engage in deep reflection

Upwards I gaze, through a light haze
Thinking of nothing as I laze
Whilst drifting into a sleepy daze

The good Lord is with me, I am at peace

CONVICTION OF SIN

While waiting for a bus to take me to a City Centre, terrible memories of a recent period of failure came flooding back into my mind. Feeling utterly crushed inside, I said to myself:

I too am afflicted with total depravity
It is not a remote doctrine
Far removed from everyday life.
At times my whole being hates God
With a full-blooded intensity
My will wants to kill Him.
My reason despises Him
My emotions fear Him
My tongue maligns Him

To me it seems that
Christianity is an unattractive fairy tale
An unreal myth
A cruel lie
Enticing me to disaster

Where now is the great promise of salvation?
Everything in me
Is completely wrong
Totally wrong
And utterly wrong
I am a creature fit only for hell

I have found, the hard way
That *'total depravity'* can manifest itself
In proud self-images and desires
I realise that I am alienated
And too helpless to change
I am like a drowning man
Who refuses any help
For pride has been my ruin

DESIRES

Show yourself trustworthy, Jesus
Prove to your servant
That you will answer my petitions
Ensure that the evildoers will not say,
"Hah! Some God he worships,
His prayers will end-up in thin air!"

Abba Father, fulfil all my needs
Not for my sake alone
But for your glory
Relate my thoughts to reality
Show yourself through me –
Reach out to those who doubt

Possess me, Holy Spirit of God
You, who hovers above the furthest galaxies
Whose mind knows every microbe
And for whom even the sub-atomic particles dance
Please, give me more love
To help bridge the alienation
Which exists between God and Man

You see, Father
I so desire to serve you
All I have been given is yours to use
To belong to you
Is a crowning honour
So rise, come and finish the work you began
Please hear your servant's plea
As I bow my head in utter shame, Amen

DETESTING

How I detest those times when you appear absent
How I detest those times when you seem completely absent
How I detest those times when you stand aside
And let me fail

So, make haste and act, Oh Lord
Show me your grace
And grant success
In all of the endeavours
You have called me to undertake
In the name of Jesus Christ, our Lord, Amen

DRASTIC MEANS

When I used to *'sign on'* as unemployed
I nearly gave up on you Lord
In the slowly shuffling dole queue
Full of blank, despairing, resentful faces
I thought in my heart
'This is a useless God I serve,
He's brought me nothing but *'FLOP'*
F̲ailure, l̲oneliness, o̲ppression and p̲overty
He's done nothing
He says nothing
He brings nothing
In my wretched trouble-filled life
Except destitution, disillusionment and despair

Time now to ditch this ineffective, useless deity
Who promises great things and then does nothing.
He can't even provide for my family!
Time now to follow some other god
Time now to ditch Christianity and find some other saviour
Time now to repudiate this delusory faith
I once followed so fervently
I'm far better off without this Christ!

But, through drastic means
You turned me around

In your mercy, you re-directed my life
And, one step at a time
You gradually restored my fortunes
And gave as much blessing as I could cope with

In your mercy you opened doors of opportunity
Providing worthwhile employment
For this blessing, I thank you

GOD IS MY GUIDE – WHY WORRY?

God is my guide
Why worry?

I am fully open to His Holy Spirit
There is no need to fear
Great blessings shall accrue
In obedience to His will

Although I burn in the fires of tribulation
And all help seems far away
He will protect me
Teaching me many things
Amidst great suffering

In His tender hands I am safe
Ready to be restored
To enjoy fresh blessings
Which bring glory to His name

Much of my life has fallen apart
Causing me anguish and dismay
Yet my confidence in Him will be renewed
His Spirit shall re-anoint me

His great love follows me wherever I go
Giving me a victorious triumph over all of my foes
His love leads me to dwell in places of safety
Where I will be forever secure

God is my guide
Why worry?

HAVE I BEEN WRONG?

Have I been wrong
Have I been wrong
To throw myself upon God's mercy?

No I have not!

Hold fast, oh my soul
Go to His Word
Study His providence
Remember His great deeds
And continue trusting in His mercy

I will not be afraid to appear before Him
In my weakness
I believe that, in due time
He will lift me up

HOW LONG?

How long?
How long, Oh God
Must I await your deliverance
From my situation?

Why do you hold back your blessing
Are you reneging on your promises?
Will there be no good news at all?
Is there nothing constructive planned?

Lord, Lord
<u>Do</u> something!
If you don't act
My whole vocation will be finished
Don't let me fall at the final hurdle
Don't allow everything to collapse at the last minute
Oh God, don't let me be ruined by defeat

Lord, how long must this agonizing wait continue
Before you provide a definite answer to my prayers?
Are you not faithful to your Word?
Are you not to be trusted?
Are you not able to honour your promises?

Of course you are more than able, Lord
<u>Because you say so</u>
<u>And because your Bible says so</u>
And because I have seen your acts of mighty intervention
At certain times in my own life
But how long is it before you will keep faith with me
And clear the way to reform your Church?

Lord! Don't you see that
After knowledge of you
The desire to be used mightily by you
To spread your kingdom on earth
Represents the deepest longing of my heart
Please hurry and begin to fulfil
These heartfelt aspirations
Let the work you do through me be awe-inspiring

I SEEK

I seek you Jesus
And long for more of you
Yet, when I don't seem to find you
Life has no meaning
I get bitter and frustrated
And begin chasing after other gods
To fill the space
That you alone should fill

IN MONASTERY GARDENS

In a monastery garden, I sat:
Expecting
Praying
Seeking
The presence of God

Beside a monastery rose bed, I sat:
Searching
Hunting
Desiring
The presence of God

Beneath a monastery plum tree, I sat:
Enjoying
Receiving
Soaking in
The presence of God

Oh, how good it is!

IN QUIET CONFIDENCE

When sin overwhelms me

All I can do
Is look to your grace

When wild passions rage in my soul

All I can do
Is look to your grace

When dark thoughts trouble my mind

All I can do
Is look to your grace

When enticing temptations beguile my heart

All I can do
Is look to your grace

When everything appears to fall apart

All I can do
Is look to your grace

When many troubles beset my life

All I can do
Is look to your grace

When evildoers issue their angry threats

All I can do
Is look to your grace

In quiet confidence, I look to your grace
Because I know that you, Jesus, died for me
And dealt with all of my sins
Alleluia

IT WAS THROUGH MERCY

It was through mercy
That God spared my son
So that the lump above his groin
Turned out to be a harmless cyst
For He is the Lord
The giver, preserver and taker of life
Who moulds everything to fulfil His purpose

It was through mercy
That He gave me and my wife
A healthy child to love and cherish
To bring him up in ways which are true
So that, through him
Others may be blest

It was through mercy
That God spared us the pains of bereavement
Convicting me of sin
Pushing me into repentance
And causing me to cry out to Him

It was through mercy
That God has given me
A fresh appreciation
Of the lives of my young children
So deepening my care for them
And strengthening the practical side of my nature
Whilst granting me the grace to give out to others

Yes God
You are He
Who blesses others
Through the closely-knit families
Of your people
May you who formed me in the womb
Give me the grace to respond to your mercy
By showing mercy

LET DOWN: A WRITER'S LAMENT

A wretched, useless writing life
Has amply displayed

'The vanity of human wishes'

The endless postponement of good news
Has made my heart grow sick
The lack of any breakthrough
Has filled me with despair

Have you let me down, oh Lord?

The lack of any positive reply
Has brought a dumb weariness of mind
I walk along a street of closed doors
Not one of which opens

Have you let me down, oh Lord?

All of my hard work
Has come to nothing
My best endeavours
Have borne no fruit

Have you let me down, oh Lord?

My many labours
Have yielded no result
I painstakingly nurtured my talents
Yet opportunities kept passing me by

Have you let me down, oh Lord?

I've published many creative pieces
But still I languish in futile obscurity
Innovative ideas have been boldly applied
Only to be lost in a delusory mist

Have you let me down, oh Lord?

Many avenues have been explored
Each one a frustrating dead-end
I've taken many calculated risks
With nothing to show for it

Have you let me down, oh Lord?

I've done my best to get somewhere
Yet, in the end, I've got nowhere
I've laboured into the early hours
All that time wasted

Have you let me down, oh Lord?

I've edged forward in quiet confidence
Only to be blocked by rejection
Each one of my aspirations
Has turned to dust

Have you let me down, oh Lord?

Long-cherished hopes
Have ended in cruel disappointment
A desire for success
Has remained unfulfilled

Have you let me down, oh Lord?

All of my keen ambitions
Now lie trampled underfoot
My most cherished dreams
Are a cruel mirage

Have you let me down, oh Lord?

My fervent expectations
Have all ended in disillusionment
My boundless enthusiasm
Has shrunk to a resentful apathy

Have you let me down, oh Lord?
A strong desire to do great things

Has been repeatedly frustrated
A craving for victory
Has ended in cruel humiliation

Have you let me down, oh Lord?

Great things have been promised
But nothing at all delivered
I trusted in your provision
But no breakthrough came

Have you let me down, oh Lord?

You led me so very far
Only to leave me in a wilderness
A craving to be used by you
Has always been thwarted

Have you let me down, oh Lord?

Your promises of guidance
Are hollow and meaningless
I prayed fervently to you
But no clear answer came

Have you let me down, oh Lord?

I cried out to my Creator
But you responded with an impenetrable silence
I was honest in my complaints
But you turned a deaf ear

Have you let me down, oh Lord?

A longing for fellowship with you
Has been met with only cold indifference
My attempts to follow you
Have led me into a desert

Have you let me down, oh Lord?

The Spirit's blessings

Have ceased to flow
I'm stuck fast in a *'slough of despond'*[56]
With no one to pull me out

Have you let me down, oh Lord?

I want you to draw near
But you're so far away
I long to hear you speak
But you remain coldly silent

Have you let me down, oh Lord?

I'm now of mature years
And nothing has come of my life
In old age I hope to provide for my wife
But now destitution beckons

Have you let us down, oh Lord?

Arise! Stir yourself and act!
Move, and once more <u>be</u> the God of victories
Come and use your miraculous power
To save me from perishing
In the howling, skull littered wilderness
That is failure, Amen

PROGRESSION

First, see God in scripture
Then progress to see Him in other people
From there, go on to see Him in your circumstances
And then you will be ready to receive direct guidance from Him

---

[56] A deep bog in John Bunyan's famous allegory, *'The Pilgrim's Progress'*

PRUNING

Lord, is there no encouragement for me in this?

'For you,
This is not a time of encouragement
But it is a time of pruning[57]
I will give you
An abundance of encouragements
Later on.'[58]

Oh God
Am I not your child?
Are you not my Father?
Did you not send Jesus to die for me?
Have you not sealed me with your Holy Spirit?
Then why do you withhold your blessing?
Why do my requests seem to fall upon deaf ears?
Why are my efforts in prayer to no avail?

Why does your hand lie heavy upon me?
Where now is the fulfilment of your words –
Is your wrath going to stay on me?
Am I a creature fit only for condemnation –
A candidate for the pit who has no hope?

Crushed by failure
Worn out by continual adversity
I cannot help but question
Whether your promises of help really do exist?

Will you keep faithful to your word?
Surely, you're nothing like a politician
Who makes attractive offers one day
Only to withdraw them the next?

---

[57] A *'pruning'* of what turned out to be areas of wilfulness in my life
[58] By Christmas of that year these had started to come in the form of Educational work and other encouragements, (Deuteronomy 18:22)

I see wicked ministries thrive
Whilst I am left to languish
In obscurity and failure
'False' ministries are applauded in your Church
Whilst true ones are despised and rejected
Left to flounder in their own abject helplessness
Are you really surprised at my bitterness of heart?

Where now are the words of the Holy One?
Oh God, you seem so damn ineffectual!
You don't appear to have much capacity
To sort out the Church –
Never mind the world!

I then paused, once more, in order to listen, only to find that I was left with nothing but my own internal desolation *'Punished by silence'* I bitterly reflected, *'punished by silence.'*

REVELATION AT THE DOOR

One, two, three, four
Revelation at the door

Five, six, seven, eight
Time <u>now</u> to abandon hate

Nine, ten, eleven, twelve
Into God I want to delve

One, two, three, four
My desire is to know much more

Five, six, seven, eight
Following Jesus, is now my happy fate

Nine, ten, eleven, twelve
Got to die to all of self

One, two, three, four...

THE DEVOTED

God is with us
In all the good works we do
For He is the source and enabler of every righteous deed
Deeds which He brings to full completion

In all our care
In all our patience
In all our love
Jesus is present

Each time we visit the sick in hospital
He is there in us
Relieving their abject loneliness

Each time we bring comfort to the bereaved
He is there in us
Offering them great compassion

Each time we rebuke the wicked
He is there in us
Confronting them in their sin

Each time we do simple, practical, helpful things
He is there in us
Accomplishing much needed, useful tasks

Each time we manifest the gifts of His Spirit
He is there in us
Welling up from the depths of our being

Yes, He offers endless grace and encouragement
To all who are devoted to Christ
This is because He is the God
Of infinite love and perfect creativity

End Notes

Dates following the title show when each piece was first drafted.

A Cry for Deliverance Monday 6th September 1976, whilst under physical attack from an evil spirit. This took place in the ground floor study room of a Christian Guesthouse on Holy Island, Northumbria. The words from *"outpour"* to *"Amen"* had already formed in my mind late the previous August whilst praying to the Lord in Saint Jude's Church, Earls Court, London. At that time I was in an utterly dreadful emotional state. I was becoming aware that absolutes of good and evil did exist. This *'Cry for Deliverance'* was repeated the following Thursday evening when another demonic incursion produced much poltergeist activity seen in the flashing of a strange orange light. The effect of these formative experiences was to *'blow apart'* the secular world view I had hitherto been clinging onto – despite my sudden conversion to Christianity during the previous October. It also left me with the conviction that this ordeal had been allowed to happen in order to prepare me to confront some future crisis in the Church. These events were so traumatic that I endured regular mental flashbacks until 1986. An edited version of this prayer is found in the seventh and eighth responses of Section 24 of *'The Leeds Liturgy.'*

Bit-by-Bit: Tuesday, 1st November 1990. This internal dialogue alludes to the gradual, stage-by-stage building of His Kingdom in the hearts and minds of those who follow Him.

Cloud Watching: Saturday, 5th September 2009 whilst staying at a certain Anglican Religious House. Earlier that afternoon, I'd been lying on the garden grass, thinking of nothing in particular.

Conviction of Sin: Tuesday, 10th March 1981, at a time when everything appeared to have fallen apart in my life. *'Conviction of Sin'* refers to the Holy Spirit's work in exposing sin and convincing people that they are helpless sinners, in desperate need of divine mercy. This doctrine of *'Total Depravity'* teaches that every single part of us is twisted up by sin. This term was used to convey the ugliness of what I was thinking.

Desires: Late 1977 (or early 1978) and written on some college notes during a boring lecture. It expresses the desire

for God to show His trustworthiness in times of doubt. It was actually rediscovered on a very tatty piece of paper whilst sorting through some old Sociology notes on Thursday, 8th February 1990.
Detesting: Friday, 19th February 2010.
Drastic Means: Saturday, 7th October 2006. It expresses the way personal failure can tempt one to unbelief.
God Is My Guide – Why Worry? April 1976. It expresses confidence in God's guidance throughout a time of great emotional turmoil.
Have I Been Wrong?: Monday, 3rd September 1990 whilst on retreat and desperately worried about my lack of employment as the British economy was entering a recession. Despite recently obtaining a useful Diploma in Management Studies, my life appeared to have run into a complete dead-end. Biblical promises that God would meet my needs seemed utterly untrue. I was persevering in my faith through gritted teeth.
How Long?: Monday, 3rd September 1990. It expresses the need to call upon God when in a state of despair. Sadly, by 2012 I finally concluded that the Churches in the UK were irreformable. Happily, within a month of writing this prayer I'd gained employment – thus bringing this crisis of faith to an end. At the time I was awaiting replies to job applications which never seemed to come.
I Seek: Friday, 27th October 1978. It first came to mind whilst waiting (in a torrential evening shower) for an overdue bus at South Shields. It expresses the frustrations which may be encountered on our spiritual journey.
In Monastery Gardens: Saturday, 5th September 2009 in the rose garden of *'The Community of the Resurrection,'* an Anglican Religious House where I was staying and undertaking much private study.
In Quiet Confidence: Monday, 15th November 2010
It Was Through Mercy: Thursday, 30th January 1986, ten days after hearing that a lump found in my eldest son's groin had not been malignant. It had first formed in my mind during the previous Tuesday evening, whilst praying over my son as he lay asleep. (Twelve days prior to this my middle son had been born.)
Let Down, A Writer's Lament: Thursday, 8th October 2009, when all attempts at having my books published

appeared to have failed. Any writer having experienced the treadmill of making submissions to publishers will be able to identify with this poem. In the end, I decided to publish my work independently. By early 2019, some limited recognition was finally being gained in the form of limited sales, positive reviews and speaking engagements . It had taken thirty-three years of effort to reach this point. Near the poem's beginning, reference is paid to another long poem, *The Vanity of Human Wishes'* (written by Dr Samuel Johnson, 1709-1784). I purchased a copy of this work whilst visiting the Johnson Museum in Gough Square, London on Friday, 18th September 2009. It was a highly moving piece and I found its sentiments matched my own.

Progression: Wednesday, 4th October 1989.The main theme expressed here is the need to discern God's voice in scripture before hearing from Him through other means. (However, this is not to deny that, in His gracious mercy, He may occasionally speak in a direct manner to believers – especially when there's a definite need to be met.)

Pruning: Friday, 31st August 1990. Written at a time of great depression – in part caused by the threat of unemployment. It shows how suffering often forces people to ask questions about God and His ability to help. Reference is made to the ministries of John Wimber and the Kansas City Prophets which were enjoying a wave of popularity at the time this meditation was written. I was severely tempted to envy their apparent popularity and success. The way they were made to look fools (by the failure of their prophecy predicting that revival would breakout within the UK during October 1990) promptly cured me of that particular temptation!

Revelation at the Door: Tuesday, 3rd July 1990, after it had re-emerged whilst walking through a city centre. It had originally come to mind in late October 1975, shortly after my sudden and exciting conversion to Christianity.

The Devoted: Friday, 29th November 1985. It expresses how God can work through the good deeds of His people. There is, of course, no intention to teach *'justification by works.'* Rather, it is assumed that such deeds <u>follow</u> from the new life to be found in Christ. The need for faith is clearly shown elsewhere in this work.

ACT 7: THE COMING

SCENE 1: THE JUDGEMENT

Numbers 16:31b-32, *"The ground under them split asunder and the earth opened her mouth and swallowed up the households of* [the rebellious] *Korah, along with all their men and all their goods."*

ACCURSED

Accursed are they
Who rely upon charms
To protect them from the evil one
Foolish are they
Who put their trust in amulets
Hoping for the *'evil eye'* to spare them
Meanwhile, demons look on
And, amongst themselves they gloat:

"They are afraid of us
They acknowledge our power
And recognize our authority.
Let us go and increase oppression
Let us haunt them through the night
And torment them through the day
Let us plague their minds with fear
And rob their hearts of hope."

Yes, foolish are they
Who place their confidence
In magical means of protection
For such means act as a magnet
To emissaries from the evil one
Better to put one's trust
In the Lord of heaven and earth

Cleave to the Lord Jesus Christ
And you will be saved
From the judgement to come

Believe firmly in His atonement at Calvary
Where He gained the redemption of your sins
And prised loose the grip of the evil one
Better to have faith in Christ
Then in any craven superstition

ANGUISH

So much lying
So much deceit
So much pride
So much defeat
So much arrogance
So much despair
Everything seems beyond repair

Things have now come to a head
The earth is laid waste
The land is parched but the seas rage
We exist in an era of global torment
Supplies are at an end
And no hope is left

Oh, how I wish that I were dead
For I have no wish to exist
As a destitute failure
Living on memories of a prosperous yesterday

Oh Lord!
Give me success or give me death
Remember the blood of your Son
And answer this prayer
Amen!

CALAMITY

When catastrophe looms over the land
And the whole earth is stricken with judgment
Those who abused the Lord with empty words
Will say:
"What fools we've been,
We scoffed at God
Making it a regular habit
To blaspheme His name
And now calamity has befallen us!"

Bitterly they think ...

Why did we jeer at Him
Whom we did not know?
Why did we laugh so contemptuously at Jesus
Who is now our judge?
Why did we swear and curse the name
Which should have been our salvation?"

Their hearts are afire with self-condemnation
(Though hardened against the truth)
They will tremble at the sound of God's voice
To them, Christ's return will be a terrible harbinger of doom

The earth shakes and cracks open

The earth shakes and the cracks become deep trenches

The earth shakes and the deep trenches become yawning chasms into which the blasphemers fall

The earth shakes
It closes up
To swallow the blasphemers
Who are no more

FROM DUST TO LIFE

Part A: Dust

Early one Sunday Morning
I lay in bed
Half asleep and half awake
And dreamt I was trudging through
A lifeless landscape
Littered about with: -
Ruined buildings
Scorched fields
And the charred bones
Of dead farm animals
To my left
Lay a brackish putrid-smelling sea
That bubbled away menacingly
Many dead fish floated
On its foam flecked waves
Above it stood a high chalk cliff
Dotted about with myriads of empty nests
Where once thousands of birds
Had dwelt
Now all was silent

I walked slowly
Along a sandy, undulating path
Toward a small ruined settlement
Noticing how the signs of burning
Grew more marked
As I approached it
On peering at this desolate scene
I quickly gathered
That this place
Had suffered a terrible
Environmental and/or nuclear disaster
I seemed to have entered a time portal
Which had taken me
Into an awful future
Inside a world
Ruined by a human-generated cataclysm

On glancing upwards
I saw billowing, black clouds
Concealing a blood red moon
A dim hazy sunlight
Hovered around a blackened horizon
A sickly, sulphurous smell
Wafted up my nose
Adding further to my discomfort

Meanwhile, a howling wind
Ruffled my hair,
And blew dust into my face
It created an unpleasant grittiness in my eyes
And a sooty taste in my mouth
My breathing became laboured
As phlegm filled my tightening throat
I seemed to be on the verge
Of having an asthmatic attack
After coughing loudly
I shook my head in despair whilst reflecting
This is utterly apocalyptic
Death pervades the planet!
Higher life forms seem extinct
What has happened?'

Before I moved on
I noticed, lying at my feet
A skeletal hand
Clinging to a battered computer tablet
Imprinted on a remnant of brown skin
Was some kind of mark or tattoo
So faded it was barely legible
Out of curiosity I picked up the tablet
And as I did so the hand crumbled into fine dust
I jumped back involuntarily
Startled and shocked to the core
I found myself staring transfixed at the *'tablet'*
Which I now held in my left hand
I pressed a button
And the screen flickered into life
Against a bright turquoise background
Screamed the headline:

WORLD PEACE DAY CELEBRATION COMING SOON!
BILLIONS EXPECTED TO WATCH KEY EVENTS USING THE LATEST QUANTUM APS
- Title: The Onward Triumph of Humanity
- Message: Safeguarding the World from Disaster
- World Teacher Expected to Work his Magic
- Art and science displays will highlight the need for unity

Mass Attendance Expected

Using the latest techniques
In Social Mathematics
Experts claim that World Peace Day Three
Will draw an attendance of billions
Scientific and artistic displays
Will illustrate the new Global values
Of Justice, Peace and Love.
Presiding over this event
Will be our Dear World Teacher
Who will display his usual Charisma
Senior religious and political leaders
From all communities
Will assuredly pledge
Their whole-hearted allegiance
When conferring upon him the title
'King of Kings'

Quantum Solutions

An important theme will be
'Safeguarding the world from disaster.'
Informed sources claim that both
Quantum and spiritual solutions
To current climatic and ecological challenges
Will be revealed by our beloved leader
In his role as *'Prince of Peace'*
He will once more highlight the need
For Global *'Unity'*

A Giver of Hope

The ecstatic devotion
'The God of Our Age' attracts
Reflects his radical inclusivity.
He has openly promised
That, under his global rule
All humanity will be given the capacity
To ascend to a higher spiritual plain
And attain perfect Deity

On offer is the promise to gain access
To hitherto secret knowledge
The humblest citizen
Will become like God
Able to discern what is good or evil
Fears that all of this simply reflects
A dangerous religious megalomania
Have proved unfounded

Our dear teacher continues to astound expert commentators
By the humility he displays
When performing great wonders.
In recent negotiations
He charmed the most sceptical
Of political leaders into accepting his divinity
Whilst offering a New Age
Of *'Hope and aspiration*
One observer disclosed
'The love he radiated
Was simply awesome
He would stride into the room'
And we would feel it
The power was overwhelming
There was incredible personal magnetism
He …'

With a buzz the screen went blank
It took a violent shake for it to come to life again
On the screen there appeared a hymn of praise

HYMN FOR WORLD PEACE, DAY THREE

He came and gave us life
By ending all worldly strife
His peace will never cease
His love will forever increase

A re-greening of Gaia[59] has finally begun
His Kingdom has now truly come
Our many fears he has utterly vanquished
Our weighty cares – all have vanished

A tired old *'Secular Order'* has been displaced
Failed messiahs have been replaced
You soar into higher realms, oh mighty Lord –
Over the world your love has been outpoured!

Oh, you are the bright morning star
Your shining beauty radiates near and far!
You are the much-loved light-bearer
Who's made the world so much fairer

You are our dear, exalted Saviour
Who gives life a very sweet flavour
Angels of light follow your train
Helping to secure your glorious reign

A grim death will no longer be
It's something we will <u>never</u> see
You fulfil our wildest, happiest dreams
Your glory is one of our many themes

Accompanied by a loud rendering
Of Handel's Hallelujah Chorus
A picture then appeared showing children
From all nations
In colourful attire
Some were seated
Whilst others stood

---

[59] An Ancient Greek term in which the Earth is personified as a Goddess. *'Mother Earth'* would be a correct, if rather loose, translation.

Holding paper lanterns
Atop long red poles
A look of gleeful excitement
Beaming from their faces
Hanging from chains
Around their necks were crosses
But not the crosses associated with Christianity
Rather, the broken cross of The Peace Movement

An even louder buzz
The screen goes blank once more

After three failed attempts
To shake it back to life
I thrust this wretched device
Into my left trouser pocket
And resumed my journey
Bitterly reflecting on how the grand hopes
Of humanity had once more come to nothing.
Mankind's history had still ended
In a massive global holocaust
Despite the gimmick of *'World Peace Days.'*
I sadly concluded that the Earth's population
Had been seduced by a great
but especially attractive delusion –
One with the capacity to appeal
To our strongest desires

When I cautiously approached
Some fire-gutted buildings
I saw separate piles of blackened ash and dust
Containing what appeared to be tiny slithers of bone
I grimly wondered
Whether these were the cremated remains
Of incinerated individuals
As the wind strengthened
Each pile of dust
Formed mini-eddies and tornadoes
Pirouetting like dancing ghosts
Over small piles of rubble

On watching this desolate scene
I anxiously wondered
This is horribly bleak
Why am I seeing this?
OK I get it!
This false messiah
Will almost destroy humanity
His reign will end
In mass death
And destruction.
But that's in scripture anyway
So why am I here?'

The wind began to ebb away
And the dust and ashes drifted down
Silently landing on the ground
Then something strange happened
As I continued to look
The ashes and dust began to settle
Into the shape of definite human bodies
I could just make out
The featureless heads
Torsos and limbs
They each resembled the sandmen
That children make on beaches
'So they were people after all!
Poor blighters – they didn't stand a chance
Let's hope their end came quickly.'

Then with a start ...

Part B. Life

I heard a loud voice from Heaven shouting
'Let there be life!'

At once the ashes and dust coagulated
Into clean, ivory-white bones
With a noisy rattle they joined-up
To form perfect human skeletons
Quickly, I grasped the whole process
Of death was being reversed

Life was being formed from the dust
What I appeared to see
Was an act of re-creation
God's making of Adam
Came into mind
Was this act of creation
Being re-enacted
On a global scale?

Muscles swept over the bones
Followed by a blanket of skin
Hair sprung from the head
(And in some cases
Beards from the chin)
Until several perfect human shapes were formed

In open-mouthed astonishment
I looked more closely
To discover that each body
Had been clothed in a white robe
They were male and female
And some seemed to be children
Individual differences
Were also noticeable

Suddenly, from Heaven
came another loud cry
'Be still!'

The turbulent black clouds above me dispersed
Leaving only one large white cloud
Billowing in a blue sky
The Moon was no longer blood red
But had taken on a bright silver hue
And a golden sun was rising over the horizon
The wind had dropped
And the air had grown clearer and pure
There was no longer any irritation
In my nose or throat
It seemed rather symbolic
That a resurrection was poised to take place
At the dawn of a new day

The scene changed
I saw gathered together
Beneath an enormous heavenly altar
A vast array of white-robed saints
Eagerly waiting to enter
Their new resurrection bodies
Thereby finding completion
In the physical
As well as the spiritual realm
They seemed to bubble with excitement
These were a people
Who clearly delighted
In the Lord Jesus Christ
Whom they worshipped
As *'The Word Made Flesh'*

Then I saw the spirits
Of these saints
Appear above their reconstructed bodies
And glide gently into them
For a brief while
They remained still
As if in a deep sleep

Then suddenly …
I heard the booming words
'Come forth!'
This command was accompanied
By a prolonged blast
Of what sounded like
A Jewish shofar trumpet

In response
The bodies stood-up
With a plop!
Some emerged from a now calm sea
Others burst from underground holes
That had opened-up
Yet were not dirty
It was as if the earth
Couldn't hold them

Their reactions were interesting
A few rubbed their eyes
As if emerging from a deep sleep
Others gazed in wonder
At their healthy new limbs
But most simply stood there
With ecstatic smiles
Evidently feeling they were now complete
In the Lord Jesus Christ
Whom they gladly acknowledged as being
At the centre of their lives
'Marvellous' I sighed
'This resurrection marks a beginning and not an end,
May, one day, I be among these Saints!'
But it was evident
That I was witnessing
Only a tiny part of a huge phenomenon
Which was taking place
Across the whole world
Where Saints were rising
From their place of interment
And countless graves were being emptied

There was another loud blast of the trumpet
And I saw two winged angels
Appear beside each newly risen saint
Then one more blast
And the command *'come up here!'*
The Angels grasped each arm
Of a risen Saint
(If a child, they were gently
Carried by just one Angel)
Together, and with great speed
They soared upwards
Into the white cloud
Which then completely vanished
Leaving behind an empty sky
I realized that they had
All had been taken
To re-unite with Jesus
On His return to Earth

Whilst pondering these things
The earth shook violently
Such was the strength of this quake
That I fell forward onto the ground
'So he's landed'
I found myself thinking, somewhat frivolously
After a couple of minutes I stood up
Brushed some dust from my jacket
And looked around

Again, I gawped in amazement
Although the contours of the land
Were still recognizable
<u>Much had changed!</u>
The fields were now lush
With grass and trees
Healthy farm animals
Were contentedly feeding
I looked to my left
And saw what appeared to be
Several dolphins
Playfully diving in and out of a calm sea
The cliffs were crowded
With gently chirruping birds of every description
Ahead of me
Was a black and white dog
Playing happily with a ginger cat
Interestingly, whilst some buildings
Had completely vanished
Others had been restored and cleaned
As if waiting for new inhabitants

From the sky I heard
An angelic choir
Chanting the words of Luke 2:14
*"Glory to God in the Highest
And on Earth peace and goodwill towards men"*
'That's beautiful' I exclaimed
*'Creation itself has been restored
By direct, divine command. Incredible!
What a privilege it is to see this sight'*

A buzz from my pocket
Prompted me take out the tablet
I found it had been miraculously restored
To a brand-new condition
It was no longer battered and dented
But clean and shiny looking
I noticed how its frame
Had a golden rather than a rusty hue
On flicking over to the screen
I saw, erupting from the sky
Our Lord – in all of His majestic glory
He rode a snorting, white war horse
And was clothed in a blood red robe
"His eyes were as flames of fire
And on His head were many crowns …
On His robe and on his thigh
A name was written
KING OF KINGS
AND LORD OF LORDS." (Revelation19:12a & 16)
Charging behind Him
Were *"Many thousands of His Saints*
To execute judgement on all" (Jude 14b-15a)
Like our Lord Himself
They rode on white horses
But they were clothed
In *"fine white and clean linen."*
I could see this was Jesus
In the guise of a militant warrior
Coming to judge a world
That had prostituted itself
before the anti-Christ
For many surviving inhabitants
It would be a day of doom –
A case of discovering the truth
After it was too late
To do them any good.
The time for mercy and grace was over
The door of salvation
Had now been firmly shut
A period of divine wrath was beginning
And it was terrifying to behold!

Missiles of every description
Filled the sky
All were aimed to prevent our Lord's return
Yet, at His command
They fell with a clatter onto the ground
Or exploded harmlessly in mid-air
I could see how His word acted like a sword
Breaking the resistance of His many enemies.
However, I was saddened to see
That hatred of Jesus still continued
Even at His return.
There seemed to be no end of antagonism
Directed towards Him
What remained of the earth's population
Was still in open rebellion against Him
On gazing at these events
It dawned on me
How these computer tablets
Made it possible
For *'every eye to see Him.'*
Technology had helped to
Fulfil Revelation 1:7a

Then the scene shifted again
I saw our Lord with two Angels
Descending to the Mount of Olives
As soon as His feet touched the ground
A violent earthquake took place –
Splitting the mountain in two
And forming a deep valley.
Through it, a fast-flowing river
Of clear bubbling water began to flow
Geography itself
Was being re-arranged
At our Lord's coming.
I then saw new buildings
(Including a temple
Modelled on Biblical design)
Spring-up from what had been
A burnt out, war-shattered city
Darkly overshadowed by thousands

Of fat carrion birds.
One glance from the Lord
And they dispersed
With a fearful, noisy squawking

I gazed in wonder on this vista
Seeing how trees and vegetation
Were quickly springing back to life
Some of the trees were covered
With beautiful white, red and pink blossom
Natural processes were being accelerated
Vegetation that would normally
Take days or weeks to grow
Was springing-up within seconds
It was apparent that
Healing was being brought
To the devastated land of Israel

Whilst watching this
I desperately longed
To be in close proximity
With the risen, glorified Jesus!
Oh, what questions I would ask Him!
But the time for that
Had not yet come
My mind was functioning well
But what I had witnessed
Was so awesome
That, for once, words almost failed me
All I could do was mutter
'Glory be to thee, Oh Lord
May one day I be with you!
Come soon, Lord Jesus
Come soon!"
Then, invisible hands
Held my shoulders firmly
And tugged me back
Along a dark time portal
Almost instantaneously
The scene shrank and dissolved
I awoke from my dream
Knowing it had given me

Much to reflect upon.
I decided to record
The marvels that I'd seen
After all, what else could I do?

GOOD AND EVIL

What is evil?
It is destruction
Uncontrolled
And unnecessary destruction
Its end is eternal death
In the Lake of Fire

What is good?
It is construction
Edifying
And loving construction
Its end is eternal life
In the New Jerusalem

Why is pride evil?
It destroys compassion

Why is humility good?
It builds up compassion

Why is war evil?
It destroys whole nations

Why is peace good?
It develops whole nations

Why is lust evil?
It leads to gross immorality

Why is love good?
It leads to patient self-control

Why is anger evil?
It destroys relationships

Why is patience good?
It builds up relationships

Why is idolatry evil?
It weakens the soul

Why is faithfulness good?
It strengthens the soul

Why is hatred evil?
It ruins the character

Why is compassion good?
It develops the character

Why is revolution evil?
It destroys society

Why is reformation good?
It improves society

Why is Atheism evil?
It destroys the ability
To love God

Why is Theism good?
It creates the ability
To love God

ℋ 12

There are <u>three</u> hellish *Hs*[60]

H1 for Heresy
H2 for Hesitancy
H3 for Hypocrisy

All leading to …

H4 for Hatred
H5 for Horror
H6 for Hell

In contrast, there are <u>three</u> heavenly *Hs'*

H7 for Honesty
H8 for Humility
H9 for Humanity

All leading to …

H10 for Happiness
H11 for Holiness
H12 for Heaven

Two sets of *Hs'*
Two opposite ways to go
Two paths in life to follow

Now choose between them

---

[60] Pronounced *'Haitches'*

HOW LOST

How lost the wicked are
Without Christ

How futile
Are their ways

How empty their talk
Laced with pointless obscenities

How obsessed
With the things that defile

How twisted their thinking
With futile speculation

How stubbornly closed
To all appeals to reason

Abandoned
Doomed
Forsaken

Every idol they chase
Every folly they pursue
Every crime they glory in
Eternal anguish is their destiny
Where demons will be their doleful company
Unless they repent and, through faith
Receive the forgiveness (and other benefits)
Of Christ's sacrificial death upon the cross

Dear God, give me compassion for the lost
And the grace to reach them with your Gospel, Amen

OURS WAS THE FOLLY

Ours was the folly
And we were the fools

So contemptuous were we of the truth
That we failed to recognize the claims of Jesus
To us He was unimportant
A myth from long ago –
An utter irrelevance our to daily lives
We were too busy
Each of us going our own way
With pleasure as our only goal

We failed to take-up the offer of salvation
Whilst it was there to be had
We followed the way of rebellion
Hating God as a despot
We vainly substituted our own idea of righteousness
Rather than accepting the pure righteousness
Given by Jesus alone
We filled our hearts with empty, dead things
To fulfil its basest desires
We paid no regard to others –
Unless we could use them for our own gain
We chased after every useless thing
Resisting the Spirit who gives life

Ours was the folly
And we were the fools

So now we stand before Him
He who should have been our Lord
Enthroned in holiness and might

Yes, we look at Him who is now our judge
Whom we despised
Whose warnings we ignored
Whose healing we rejected

Now, unable to flinch
Or draw back

We long to hide from His purity
The books are closed
The Spirit is showing us all of our sins
The angels have gathered in solemn council
And sentence is being passed
The verdict is fair
For we are unfit to dwell with a Holy God
Yes, we have become as less than nothing
All that was good
All that which gave us pleasure
Has been stripped away

The light of truth is unbearable to our eyes
And all that remains is
An eternity of pain
An eternity without hope
Without love
Without God
An eternity spent sharing
In Lucifer's endless misery

Healing we refused
And now we are lost
There is no *'second chance'*
For the verdict is final
And the verdict is fair

Through a proud self-centredness
We have cut ourselves off
From the love of God
Now there is no hope of restoration
Already, the darkness is gathering
Toward an endless night

Ours was the folly
And we were the fools
Ours was the folly
And we were…

WHAT GOOD?

What good, Oh Father
What good would it do you
If I perished in hell?
What good is it to you
If I am numbered among the damned?
What good would it be to your Son
If you allowed me to perish in the raging fires of Hell?

How can your love be fulfilled
If you cast me forever from your presence?
How can your grace be honoured
If I am hurled into the bottomless pit?
How can your mercy express itself
If you consign me to a lost eternity?

Will not your Son have died in vain?
Will not His sufferings have been of no account?
Will not His blood sacrifice have been futility itself?
For His sake have pity on me!
Apply the benefits of Yeshua's blood sacrifice
In my life
And, out of your love for Him
Justify me in your presence
Fill me with your Spirit
And grant me the gift
Of eternal fellowship with you

For His sake alone
Pour out your love, power and grace
Honour your Son
By granting me the redemption
He alone accomplished
Respect the work He did
In blotting out my sins
And in *'remembering them'* no more!

Come, Abba Father
Please stop being absent
For an absent God is no God at all!
Please fulfil the gracious promises of your Scriptures

And rescue me
From those who rage against you
Delight your Son
By sending your Holy Spirit
To enter my life afresh
May your Son be exalted
And your Spirit honoured by the work
You will accomplish through me, Amen

End Notes

Dates following the title show when each piece was first drafted.

Accursed: Monday, 1st December 1986. It emphasises the need to rely solely upon Jesus to provide spiritual protection.

Anguish: Monday, 2nd April 2012, when facing financial ruin because of a huge downturn in my work. It was also the month that my relationship with the Churches broke down

Calamity: Monday, 27th February 1989 during the height of the Salman Rushdie affair. It is set in the time of Christ's return. Highlighted is the wonderful security which is to be found in Christ. Followers of Jesus can safely leave it to God to judge unrepentant blasphemers, with no need for the burning of books, or the issuing of death threats. In fact, to do so would be to take God's judgments into one's own hands – which is the sin of presumption.

From Dust to Life: Sunday, 7th April 2019. It first occurred as a dream-like sequence early that morning.

Good and Evil: January 1976 and first drafted in the bedroom of a certain *'Hall of Residence'* bedroom.

H12: Friday, 1st February 2019 after looking at some numerical proverbs in the Bible

How Lost: Thursday, 5th July 2012. Just less than two years later, the prayer made at the end of this meditation began to be spectacularly answered when I was called into a completely fresh direction.

Ours Was the Folly: Monday, 3rd February 1989. It highlights the terrible self-condemnation that will torment sinners on Judgement Day

What Good? Saturday, 12th March 2016

On a further note it's worth mentioning that Salman Rushdie was an Asian-born writer whose publication of *'The Satanic Verses'* enraged the Muslim Community for its alleged blasphemies and mockery of the founder of that religion. A *'Fatwa'* [religious decree] passed by the Ayatollah Khomeini of Iran sentenced Rushdie to death. He was forced to go into hiding and was under police guard for the next ten years. The Ayatollah Khomeini died in June 1989 without the *'Fatwa'* having been rescinded.

SCENE 2: THE DELIVERANCE

Obadiah 1:17, *"But upon mount Zion shall be deliverance, and there shall be holiness."*

ANSWERED

The Lord has answered my prayer
He has wrought a mighty deliverance

Give thanks to Jesus, our great High Priest

The Lord has displayed his power
He has gained a telling victory

Give thanks to Jesus, our mighty King

The Lord has acted in love
He has displayed a wonderful compassion

Give thanks to Jesus, our teaching prophet

The Father listened to his Son
And His Spirit anointed my prayers

Give thanks to Jesus, our one true mediator

All members of the Trinity played their part
To bless the Son with the honour He deserved

Give thanks to Jesus, our one true God

BY HIS POWER

By His great power the Holy One of Israel will save you
By His merciful grace He will show you the Messiah
By the strength of His outstretched arm
He will deliver you
A people hated in the world's sight
But precious to God

Rejoice, your time of deliverance is near
Be consoled, all you who are dismayed
Be comforted, all you who fear
Be trusting, all you who doubt
And are tempted to say
"The times are bitter, there cannot be a God"

The Lord you follow
Is not a God who stands afar off
Nor is He indifferent to your needs
He takes no delight in your affliction
Instead, He is gentle, merciful and kind
Eagerly honouring the covenant
He made with Abraham
A covenant spanning thousands of years
Look and see
Peer and gaze
Observe and be amazed
For behold, it is the Lord
Who protects you
It is His Spirit
Who removes the veil
Lying over your hearts
In His love
The Lord will forgive all of your sins
And grant you a mature faith –
Your testimony will astonish the world
The promises He made in scripture
<u>Will be fulfilled</u>
What He has said <u>shall</u> be accomplished
Nothing can ever thwart His plans

Believe and trust
For the Lord is baring His mighty arm
To rescue you from your enemies
He <u>will</u> prevail
And you <u>shall be delivered!</u>

CRAVINGS

Such cravings
Such longings
Such yearnings
Who can restrain them?

Unless it be...
The almighty power of God

Such ambitions
Such emotions
Such passions
Who can reform them?

Unless it be...
The almighty grace of God

Such desires
Such drives
Such desperate needs
Who can redeem them?

Unless it be...
The almighty love of God

FAITHFUL WITNESS

To thee, oh Christ I come
To thee, oh Christ I speak
To thee, oh Christ I pray
To thee, oh Christ I listen
To thee, oh Christ I cry!

In this age of grotesque delusion
Grant me the strength and the love
To be your faithful witness
To the people you've given me, Amen

OLD TIME GOSPEL PLEA

Come now, dear reader
Give heed to this word
Let me plead with you
And show you how
To receive eternal life

Do not hunger after worldly fame
It tends only toward sorrow and pain
Do not despise God's true revelation
The result will only be devastation
Do not believe a beguiling lie
Lest in the end you shall surely die
Please do not follow a 'wrecker's light'[61]
Though its presence may be a welcome sight

You need not be left undone
Place your faith in God's only Son
There's no other saviour but Him
The light He offers will never dim
From His written Word you will deduce
That a relationship with God he <u>will</u> produce

---

[61] These were lights placed on clifftops, deceptively acting as a lighthouse, so enticing ships to crash and break-up. Local villagers would then salvage the cargo – either to sell on or use to for their own benefit.

Our Creator can be our dearest friend
His compassion for us will never end

I shall now make this Gospel plea
It's an offer made to you for free
Accept it today (rather than tomorrow)
It certainly is the best way to follow
It's the path of true Christian belief
And it's here that you will find inner relief
Flee to Jesus – your precious Saviour
Beseech Him to show you His merciful favour!

Hear now the old-time Gospel call
Allow it to undo the effect of *The Fall*
In Jesus, forgiveness can be received
On that note you will not be deceived
So make haste! Be quick! Flee to Him!
Let Him deal with your vilest sin
Believe He rose up from the grave
So sinners like us He could save

Fierce but gentle is His compassion
Our personal growth He wants to fashion
Allow Him to end your inner strife
Accept from Him a brand-new life
Through His word He speaks
To anyone who earnestly seeks
Please turn to Him if only you would
For in Him, there dwells all that is good

Oh, troubled soul, enjoy His rest
He really does know what is best
Our hearts His Spirit wishes to fill
And His presence we can be still
Our intellects He will enlighten
Our emotions He will assuredly brighten
Many blessings we will forever know
We see the defeat of our satanic foe

So, dear reader, cease to mope
In Christ, you have a certain *'hope'*
Let Him be your main attraction

Let Him inspire helpful action
Christ is God's only begotten
May that never be forgotten
And in Him place all of your faith
Then forever you will be safe, Amen

ONLY JESUS CAN

Who can bear our evil
Who can cleanse our many iniquities
Who can remove the sin
Sticking to us like industrial glue?

Only Jesus can

Then why not turn to Him for deliverance?

NO ONE!

The Lord is holy
The Lord is pure
The Lord is unapproachable
He is infinitely separate from anything profane
No one may approach the Lord
In their own strength and live!

Yet, in His love, He sent His only Son Jesus
Who came in the flesh to save us
<u>Only through His blood sacrifice</u>
<u>May we approach the Lord</u>
And avoid the wrath that is our due

VINDICATION

The Lord has vindicated our cause

Alleluia!

Our would-be destroyers have been confounded

Alleluia!

They pressed-in hard but were defeated

Alleluia!

Victory belongs to our God

Alleluia!

He honours those who are faithful to Him

Alleluia!

He comforts His hard-pressed servants

Alleluia!

Amidst many trials He comforts them

Alleluia!

May His name be glorified forever

Alleluia!

The Lord has honoured our faith

Alleluia!

This brings great joy and relief to our hearts

Alleluia!

WHAT BEGINNING IS THIS?

What beginning is this?
A beginning that will bring
Victory or defeat?
Wealth or poverty?
Love or hate?
Or …
Is it a beginning bringing none of the above?

I gaze ahead
And find the future
Is a blank piece of paper
Waiting to be written on by many hands

End Notes

Dates following the title show when each piece was first drafted.

Answered: Wednesday, June 29th 2005. A celebratory psalm eldest written on the day after my son had been granted a 2:2 Hon's Degree in Computing (multi-media). We'd been were so delighted on hearing the news (in the University Seminar Room) that we'd hugged each other, jumping up and down and punching our fists into the air! Its theme is the joy which answered prayer can bring.

By His Power: Friday, 24th January 1992. Written to emphasise how the Lord will rescue a remnant of Jewish people in Israel. This will take place during a time of armed conflict when each of the world's nations will be arrayed against Israel.

Cravings: Wednesday, 4th March 2015

Faithful Witness: Friday, 15th June 2019

Old Time Gospel Plea: Wednesday, 22nd May 2019, prompted by reading an old Methodist hymn book during my morning prayer time.

Only Jesus Can: Monday, 11th September 2006 whilst seated on a large grey rock near the top of a certain Moor. It expresses the fact that only Jesus can deal with our sinful nature; looking for an alternative remedy is a waste of time.

No One: Monday, 8th February 1999. It expresses the need to appreciate divine holiness and love.

Vindication: Wednesday, 19th December 2007. Originally written in the first-person, it expresses the inner triumph felt as evidence mounted to vindicate an unpopular stance I'd taken. This concerned the leadership of Rowan Williams, the then Archbishop of Canterbury.

What Beginning Is This? Wednesday, 17th January 2012. Written at a time when my future seemed very dark and my relations with a church were well on the way to breaking down. I remember, at the time, feeling an immense sense of disappointment in God. My Christian life appeared to have produced nothing of significance. I was desperate for some sort of new beginning in my life.(In April 2014 one did start to emerge.)

ACT 8: COMPLETION

SCENE 1: THE CELEBRATION

Psalm 149:3, *"Let them praise his name in the dance: let them sing praises unto him with the tambourine and harp."*

APPRECIATION

Oh Lord
How I appreciate
Your comforting presence
And those times
When you draw near
In your gentle love
You lead me beside still waters
To refresh my soul
And provide insight into your ways

Oh Lord
How I love you being here
How enthralled I am by your brooding presence
How I adore that sense of intimacy
When filled by your Holy Spirit

I am thrilled to bits when your incarnate word
Speaks to me
I am thrilled
By your written word

Together we enjoy one-to-one friendship
Just you and I, Abba Father
Without any distraction.
How I long for the time
When it will be possible
To enjoy such intimacy forever

How I long for the presence
Of your tender, caring Son.
My human spirit is enraptured

When in fellowship
With your invincible Holy Spirit
How He fills my frail spirit
And my whole heart!

Ah, if only things could remain this way
With me lost in the contemplation of your glory
But alas!
So many distracting duties
Make their urgent call
Upon my limited time
There's so much to do
So many tasks to perform
So much paperwork to complete
So many people to satisfy
Through the discharge of my professional duties

Yet, this time of fellowship
Between you and I
Leaves, in its wake, precious memories
May you be this close
In the last days of my life
When it's my turn
To leave this World

Please help me, dearest Father
To wisely handle this experience
Of your presence

Please help me, Lord Jesus
Never to take your love
For granted
Nor ever to treat it with scorn

Please help me, dear Spirit
To be thankful for the blessings
Of your gentle, consoling ministry

Thanks to you
My heart is at peace
I see very clearly
The way I should go

All honour, glory and power
Be to you, my sweet Holy Trinity
Now and forevermore,
Amen, Amen, and AMEN

BLESSED

God, God, God
In your perfect unity
You remain the same

Father, Father, Father,
Blessed is your name

Jesus, Jesus, Jesus
Blessed is your name

Spirit, Spirit, Spirit
Blessed is your name

Father, Father, Father
Precious is your name

Jesus, Jesus, Jesus
Precious is your name

Spirit, Spirit, Spirit
Precious is your name

Father, Father, Father
Wonderful is your name

Jesus, Jesus, Jesus
Wonderful is your name

Spirit, Spirit, Spirit
Wonderful is your name

God, God, God
In your perfect unity
You remain the same

BOND OF LOVE

Love reaches out to love
Love embraces love
Love fills-up love
Within the blessed Trinity
Where three divine Persons
Are united and filled
By a bond of unlimited love

BOUNTIFUL MERCY

Father, Father grant my prayer
Father, Father end this nightmare
Look down from Heaven and kindly act
Your help is needed - that's a fact
Bountiful, merciful, wonderful are you
Please hurry to set me free
All knowing, all loving, all powerful One
Please let your answer quickly come

BREEZY DELIGHT

How I delight in your presence
Pleasantly cooled
By the light moorland breeze
How enraptured I am
Under the space
Of a wide-open sky
Your majesty is proclaimed
In far distant hills
Your depths are exposed
In deep plunging valleys
Your strength is here
In the shining, searing sun
But strangely
It's in my heart too
In my fallen sinful rebellious heart!
It's here that you, Abba Father
Dwell most fully

BY

By the mercy of the Lord
By the greatness of His Might
I am free to live

By the arm of the Father
By the kindness of His grace
I am free to strive

By the hand of Jesus
By the compassion of His love
I am free to thrive

By the touch of His Spirit
By the strength of His anointing
I am free to drive on –
To accomplish
The perfect will of God

CELEBRATE

Adore
The Lord Jesus Christ
Who saves us through His mighty deeds

Bow
Humbly before God's holy radiance
Which shows His glory

Celebrate
The loving nature of God
In preventing us from falling

Dance
Before Abba Father
Whilst being full of His Spirit

Exalt
In those blessings
He has given to us

Listen
Intently to everything
Said in His word

Love
The mighty God
Who delivers us by His power

Rejoice
At the work
He has done amongst us

Rest
In the gentle peace
Of God, our compassionate Father

Serve
In the ministries
To which He has called us

Work diligently
To practice Your faith
In everyday life

Yield
Entirely to His will
And follow the path of humble obedience

ENRAPTURED

Our straying souls you once did capture
Which assuredly gave us eternal rapture
A new Creation we shall certainly know
Where your magnificence will be on show

What a wonderful story we can tell
Not for us the raging fires of Hell
We praise you – our dear sweet Lord
Our appreciation has greatly soared

We gather around your heavenly throne
In the New Jerusalem, which you firmly own
Sin and death have each been destroyed
In your service we are now employed

Winged cherubs chant your praise
Resounding anthems to you they raise
Your almighty power they celebrate
Your pure holiness they contemplate

Your wonderful being is truly infinite
But your grace is – oh so definite!
When we extol your royal majesty
Our hearts overflow with serenity

How awesomely great is our Creator
He gave us Jesus, our perfect saviour
Suffering and sorrow are all but past
For all of eternity our blessings will last

Such wondrous attributes make us gasp
Your tender care will hold us fast
Peace floods our hearts as we think of you
For you embody all that's good and true

Glory be to you, the great I AM
Once the perfect sacrificial lamb
In crucified agony you once bled
Need anything else now be said?

I'm too overwhelmed to say much more
Into my heart your love will pour
My feeble words are now running out
Leaving only praises for me to shout!

EVEN CLOSER

How I love being filled with your Holy Spirit
How I value this time of intimacy
How I appreciate these all too rare periods
Where we can be together, without distraction
In your presence, I'm like a lovesick nanny goat

Yet Jesus
Amidst your many blessings
I want you to draw ever closer
Please grant me further insight into your ways
And help me to apply all you've already taught me

Your presence is now so wonderful
I am lost for words
Things have moved beyond the point
Where I can say anything meaningful

Silence is now my only voice

EXALT

Exalt in the Lord, oh my soul!
For He is near
Exalt in the Lord, oh my soul!
Let Him draw close to you
Exalt in the Lord, oh my soul!
For His goodness is vast – so utterly limitless!
Trust Him to guide you
Receive His gentle Spirit
Be sustained by His great power
Give glory to Him
For He is worthy
Exalt in the Lord, oh my soul!
Yes, exalt in Him!

LET SILENCE BE MY SONG

How lovely it is to be with you, Oh Lord,
I am enraptured by your peaceful presence
Captured by the love you so gently impart
Your company is too precious for words
Fumbling poetry cannot express my delight
Rigorous analysis does not do you justice

Let silence be my song

A warm breeze gently blows around me
A symbol of your Spirit's presence
Enveloped by His blissful calm, my heart relaxes
Like a swimmer in warm still water
In quiet solitude I contemplate your mystery
'Drinking in' the green beauty of your Creation
Absorbing the majesty of your earth and sky

Let silence now speak

No barrier between you and me, oh Lord
It's just you and I together
Delighting in each other's company
Undisturbed by worldly troubles
We are joined in intimate union
You in me and I in you

Let silence spring up and shout
'God is love!
Blessed be His name forever! Amen'

LET US PRAISE HIM

God's nature is to be studied

Let us praise Him

God's existence is to be acknowledged

Let us praise Him

God's mystery is to be contemplated

Let us praise Him

God's greatness is to be pondered

Let us praise Him

God's unity is to be analysed

Let us praise Him

God's holiness is to be perceived

Let us praise Him

God's wrath is to be feared

Let us praise Him

God's judgement is to be affirmed

Let us praise Him

God's Word is to be believed

Let us praise Him

God's mercy is to be received

Let us praise Him

God's forgiveness is to be accepted

Let us praise Him

God's eternity is to be confessed

Let us praise Him

God's provision is to be enjoyed

Let us praise Him

God's sovereignty is to be followed

Let us praise Him

God's knowledge is to be respected

Let us praise Him

God's wisdom is to be trusted

Let us praise Him

God's power is to be applied

Let us praise Him

God's will is to be obeyed

Let us praise Him

God's compassion is to be celebrated

Let us praise Him

God's nature is to be adored

Let us praise Him

For His presence amongst us is a source of delight

ONE LORD

Glory to
One Lord
Divine

PRAISE YOU

Praise you Jesus:
For what you did
For what you promised
For what you suffered
For what you accomplished
For what you will do

Praise you Jesus forever
You deserve it!

SEEING YOU

In the rolling green moorland
I see you
In the hazy blue sky
I see you

In the mottled grey rock on which I sit
I see you
Left, right
Up, down,
North, South
East, West
I see you

The great Creator, Redeemer and Preserver
The God of Abraham, Isaac and Jacob
The God of kings, priests and prophets
The God of apostles, teachers and evangelists
Their God, my God, our God
Father, Son and Holy Spirit

Your beauty has been revealed
In the wonderful vastness
I see around me

TO LOFTY HEIGHTS

To lofty heights God lifts me
To whisper loving things into my ear
To disclose plans of what He is about to do
So that I will understand and follow His ways
In the service of others
Yes, to lofty heights He lifts me
To enjoy sweet communion with His Spirit
To encircle me with His love
And to fortify me for trials ahead

End Notes

Dates following the title show when each piece was first drafted.

Appreciation: Monday, 15th September 2008 expressing express delight at being in an intimate relationship with God. I was praying at the time about a major financial crisis then engulfing the world. I specifically asked, *'Lord, how should I best respond to this situation?'*

Blessed: Friday, 19th September 2008, whilst walking on a stony moorland path, enjoying a profound sense of God's presence

Bond of Love: As before

Bountiful Mercy: Monday, 13th June 2005. Its theme is the need to trust in divine mercy when praying for help.

Breezy Delight: Tuesday, 7th June 2005, whilst on a certain moor. Its theme is the sheer pleasure of rejoicing in God's presence.

By: Wednesday, 22nd September 2004. It shows how God empowers His people to accomplish His purposes.

Celebrate: Wednesday, 12th July 1990, shortly after discovering that I'd passed The Diploma in Management Studies, despite a horrendous workload. It highlights the need to rest in God before working diligently to live out the faith.

(In its original version, the first word of each verse was repeated three times for emphasis.)

Enraptured: Written on Sunday, 18th May 2019 and inspired by an old Wesleyan Hymn, entitled 'O for a Thousand Tongues' (discovered by myself in a late nineteenth century Methodist Hymn book). On reading this stirring hymn, I couldn't help but compare its fervent love of Christ with the spiritual deadness now prevalent throughout most Methodist Assemblies in the UK today

Even Closer: Friday, 19th September 2008, whilst seated on some moorland rocks. It expresses the sense of rapture which results from being near to God.

Exalt: Saturday, 22nd January 2011 whilst on a private retreat. It was followed by praying in the gift of languages.

Let Silence be my Song: Monday 10th September 2007 – whilst seated in a small hollow, (a resting stop as part of a walking day out). It expresses the joyous delight at being in God's presence.

Let us praise Him: Monday, 11th September 2006. Written whilst seated on a large grey rock, near the top of a certain Moor during a warm afternoon. It expresses how believers may respond appropriately to God's attributes.

One Lord: Friday, 9th October 2009

Praise You: Late September 1976 whilst wandering around the Anglican Cathedral of Newcastle-Upon-Tyne. A heavily edited version was incorporated in *'The Sacrifice of Praise'* Section of the Leeds Liturgy. Final modifications were made in June 2019.

Seeing You: Tuesday, 7th June 2005, whilst on a certain moor. Its theme is the way Creation can remind us of the majesty of God.

To Lofty Heights: Monday, 9th October 1989, whilst attending a Christian conference in Scotland.

SCENE 2: THE LORD OF ALL

Acts 10:36, *"The word which God sent to the children of Israel, announcing peace by Jesus Christ who is Lord of all"*

ALL PRAISE

All praise be to thee
Who from sin sets us free

In Heaven you wear a glorious crown
Your name brings endless renown

Upon the Earth embattled Saints pray
Longing for your brand-new day

When we struggle against sin it's often bitter
But through it all you make us fitter

You will reign over a whole new Creation
You'll be the object of our endless adulation

BEHOLD

Behold the Lord your God in His Word
Behold the Lord your God in His Creation
Behold the Lord your God in your circumstances
Behold the Lord your God in your relationships
Behold the Lord your God in everything that is
And your faith will not falter when the day of evil strikes

COME – GO IN

Come, go in, look and see
Taste the good things of God
Appreciate all of His attributes
Learn to follow in all of His ways

Come, go in and feast bountifully
Upon the spiritual delicacies He has to offer
Imbibe deeply of His love
Lift your hands to worship His greatness

Come, go in and explore the very depths of God
Begin a wonderful journey
That will show you many mysteries
And cause you to gain a thousand insights

Come, go in and see God in all of His beauty
Let Him enfold you in His arms
Allow Him to be your heavenly champion
Cultivate a deeply personal relationship with Him

Come, go in and open your heart to God
Permit His Spirit to speak within you
Witness how He amends your circumstances
Be amazed at the changes He has wrought in others

Come, go in and be enfolded in His welcome
You can enjoy:
His ongoing protection
His boundless generosity
And His awe-inspiring love

ELOHIM

Exalted
Love from
One
Holy
Impressive
Majestic God

FAMILIES

He is God
Who binds together
Husband and wife
Parents and children

He is God
The Creator of family life
The author of every true marriage
The originator of deeply felt romantic love

He is God
Who delights
In the sound of little ones
Happily at play

He is God
Who takes an interest in every child
Caring deeply for their progress

He is God
Whose Spirit draws near
To every legitimate act of love making

He is God
Who is present
At the procreation of every child

He is God
Who uses the blueprint of genetics
To lay down every child's character

He is God
Who governs every facet
Of family life
(Work, leisure and play
All belong to Him)

HOW GREAT

Oh Lord, how great is your Word!
It is truly beyond any reader's grasp
Who can perceive its contents?
Who can fathom its meaning?
Who can apply its instructions?
Unless first regenerated
And filled by your Holy Spirit
Sent by you and your dear Son
The Lord Jesus Christ

IN THE STILLNESS

In the heart of God there lies a stillness
That goes beyond time
That lasts for eternity
That gives perfect peace
And brings total healing
To the hearts of all Christians
Who are firmly devoted to Jesus

Within this stillness
Relax – but keep alert
Let your cares go –
But be ready to use your mind
And listen to what the Holy Spirit is saying

IT BESTOWS

This is the gift
Of eternal life
It bestows ...
Endless blessings and allows us
To enjoy God's fulsome love
In His glorious New Creation

Alleluia

This is the gift
Of eternal life
It bestows ...
Freedom from
Sin, misery and death
Isolation, loneliness and strife
Every tear is wiped away

Alleluia

This is the gift
Of eternal life
It bestows ...
Healing from
Affliction, deformity and sickness
Depression, sadness and grief
All our fears vanish

Alleluia

This is the gift
Of eternal life
It bestows ...
Liberation from all
Boredom, hatred and confusion
Confusion, dismay and doubt
In Christ we are made whole

Alleluia

This is the gift
Of eternal life
It bestows ...
An open heart and mind
To enjoy ...
Fellowship with the Father
Friendship with the Son
Fulness in the Holy Spirit
We enjoy a sweet communion with our Creator

Alleluia

This is the gift
Of eternal life
It bestows ...
New resurrection bodies
And a piercing clarity of mind
When we will see Jesus face-to-face

Alleluia

This is the gift
Of eternal life
It bestows ...
Love, joy and peace
Adoration, praise and exaltation
Our celebration will never cease

Alleluia

This is the gift
Of eternal life
It bestows ...
Creativity, insight and understanding
Completeness, perfection and wholeness
We become the people we were meant to be

Alleluia

This is the gift
Of eternal life
It bestows …
Joy, rest and happiness
Dancing, singing and worship
Around the great heavenly throne

Alleluia

This is the gift
Of eternal life
It bestows …
Everything that is good
Glorious and gracious
Wholesome, wonderful and worthy
Nothing can spoil it

Alleluia

This is the gift
Of eternal life
It bestows …
Endless fascination in our Maker
Who draws us ever deeper
Into the circle of love existing between
Father, Son and Holy Spirit
In God we find fulfilment

Alleluia

This is the gift
Of eternal life
To obtain it
Repent of your sins
And place your trust
In the Lord Jesus Christ –
For eternal life is given
Only through Him
Receive it now!

Alleluia

LIFE AND DEATH

L is for living
I is for inquisitiveness
F is for fun
E is for enjoyment

But...

D is for decline
E is for entropy
A is for anxiety
T is for termination
H is for Heaven or Hell

Life and death
Two aspects of our existence
Who can escape them?
Who indeed?

MY HEART

My heart bursts with love
It bursts with love
For you the living God

My heart bursts with love
It bursts with love
For you the dynamic Word

My heart bursts with love
It bursts with love
For you the Sacrificial Lamb

My heart bursts with love
It bursts with love
For you the tender Spirit

My heart bursts with love
It bursts with love
For you, Abba Father

My heart bursts with love
It bursts with love
For those people you have given to me

My heart bursts with love
It bursts with love
Because of <u>you</u> – the Living God

PRESENCE

In the smallest electron
In the even tinier sub-atomic particle
You Lord, are present

In the realm of the atom
In the minute realm of the photon
You Lord, are present

In the depths of the earth
In the hidden depths of the sea
You Lord, are present

In the endless flat plain
In the spectacular scenery of the mountain range
You Lord, are present

In the calm of the arid desert
In the quiet calm of the hillside lake
You Lord, are present

In the boiling, gushing lava flow
In the noisy rushing tidal wave
You Lord, are present

In the boiling waters
In the steamy bubbling geyser
You Lord, are present

In the bubbling brook
In the turbulent eddying whirlpool
You Lord, are present

In the creatures of the sea
In the flying birds of the air
You Lord, are present

In the lowest virus
In the highest mammal
You Lord, are present

In a playful dog
In a very playful pussy cat
You Lord, are present

In the activities of men
In the busy activities of women
You Lord, are present

In the thoughts of the mind
In the secret longings of the heart
You Lord, are present

In the movement of the body
In the hidden movement of the organs
You Lord, are present

In the act of sleeping
In the strenuous act of working
You Lord, are present

In the act of married lovemaking
In the holy act of nuptial intercourse
You Lord, are present

In the process of conception
In the natural process of death
You Lord, are present

In the rise of civilizations
In the terrible fall of empires
You Lord, are present

In the running of business
In the effective running of trade
You Lord, are present

In the justice of the State
In the righteous justice of the Law
You Lord, are present

In the removal of tyrants
In the forcible removal of oppression
You Lord, are present

In the giving of peace
In the gentle healing of reconciliation
You Lord, are present

In the creation of beautiful art
In the imaginative innovation of new technology
You Lord, are present

In the words of literature
In the Holy Words of Scripture
You Lord, are present

In the prayers of the believer
In the desperate prayers of the faithful
You Lord, are present

In the worship of Your people
In the celebratory praise of your children
You Lord, are present

In the sacrament of baptism
In the blessed sacrament of communion
You Lord, are present

In the preaching of the Word
In the persuasive preaching of the Gospel
You Lord, are present

In the cleansing of Christ's blood
In the thorough refining of His Spirit
You Lord, are present

In the repentance of sinners
In the sorrowful contrition of great sinners
You Lord, are present

In the confession of faith
In the humble acknowledgement of sin
You Lord, are present

In the redemption of souls
In the great salvation of lost souls
You Lord, are present

In the gifts of His Spirit
In the wonderful fruit of His Spirit
You Lord, are present

In the statements of true doctrine
In the concise summaries of good biblical teaching
You Lord, are present

In the unfolding of understanding
In the rapid advancement of wisdom
You Lord, are present

In the development of Christlikeness
In the marvellous unfolding of holiness
You Lord, are present

In the rejection of error
In the firm repudiation of heresy
You Lord, are present

In moments of success
In occasions of bitter trial
You Lord, are present

In the flowers of spring
In the balmy warmth of summer
You Lord, are present

In the fog of autumn
In the chill cold of winter
You Lord, are present

In the towering clouds
In the grey forbidding storm clouds
You Lord, are present

In the noise of the wind
In the loud crack of a thunderclap!
You Lord, are present

In the deep blue sky
In the sevenfold colour of the rainbow
You Lord, are present

In the floating dust particle
In the burning, falling meteorite
You Lord, are present

In the orbit of the earth
In the stately rotation of the moon
You Lord, are present

In the light of the planets
In the shining brilliance of the sun
You Lord, are present

In the explosion of a nova
In the massive blast of a supernova
You Lord, are present

In the power of a neutron star
In the crushing power of a black hole
You Lord, are present

In the hidden centre of a nebula
In the fathomless depths of a galaxy
You Lord, are present

In the emptiness of space
In the incredible vastness of the cosmos
You Lord, are present

In the dimensions of Time
In the unknown extent of Creation
You Lord, are present

In the Saints of Paradise
In the Highest Angels of Heaven
You Lord, are present

In the boundless reaches of eternity
In the endless extent of infinity
You Oh Lord, are present!

REJOICE

Know what a privilege it is
That God loves you
Be thankful for God's love
Praise God for His love
Rejoice in God's love
And then will flow many blessings

THE BEAUTY OF THE LORD

Let the beauty of the Lord inspire fervour
Let the beauty of the Lord inspire joy
Let the beauty of the Lord inspire praise
For the beauty of the Lord is revealed in Heaven
And may also be enjoyed upon the Earth

THE GOD OF HOLY LOVE

You are the God of *'holy love'*
The God of supreme excellence
The God of an infinite number of attributes

Your ways are beyond compare
Your deeds merit ceaseless praise
Your holiness is celebrated by a whole host of angels

Everything about You is good
There is no constraint upon Your power
Your love spans the heavens

Your Spirit is present everywhere
Your wisdom governs Creation
You know everything there is to know

Such beautiful perfection overwhelms us
Such overwhelming greatness humiliates our pride
Such realms of mystery leave us speechless

Yet –

For our sakes You chose to become small
Experiencing the helplessness of babyhood
So we could know You as *'Father'*

As a Jewish man You grew up
Only to die horribly upon the cross
To completely deal with our many sins

Even so, a guarded grave couldn't hold You
Your resurrected body testified to Your triumph
From the Heavens You sent Your Comforter

By Your grace we bear witness
That You Jesus, are our Saviour, Lord and God
The Way, the Truth and the Life

You are the object of our faith
You are our much-desired hope
You are the subject of our testimony

Now come, my friend
Be wise and get to know God
Through believing in Jesus, His Son

Heartily trust that, by His death
Jesus removed your inner guilt and sin
Have confidence that He alone gives you eternal life

Believe, without any reservation
That Jesus Christ rose bodily from the dead
And even now is actively working on your behalf

Be sure, knowing that God <u>will</u> change your life
He will cause you to be a blessing to others
In ways you couldn't even begin to expect

Enjoy the presence of God
Relax under His gentle care
Actively follow His Holy teachings

For His love for us will last forever
Amen

TRINITY

Bless you Holy Trinity
One in three
Three in one
Marvellous mystery
Sacred Deity
Glorious Unity
Amen, Amen and Amen

TRIUNE WORSHIP

Father of delight
Son of great mercy
Spirit of light

You are one
I adore you

You are my love
I celebrate you

You are my God
I worship you

WONDERFUL BLESSING

What a wonderful blessing
To dwell with our Creator
In the New Jerusalem!
A golden city of peace
Filled with many mansions

How awesome!
How incredible!
How marvellous!

What a wonderful blessing
To be gathered around the throne
Joining the cherubim
In singing endless praises
To the Lord God Almighty!

Can we ...
Grasp it?
Perceive it?
Understand it?

What a wonderful blessing
To be forever united with Jesus
Whose hair is white as snow
Whose eyes blaze like fire
And whose feet shine like polished brass

Dare we ...
Probe His mysteries?
Fathom His depths?
Explore His heights?

What a wonderful blessing
To drink clear, cool water
From the River of Life
That flows from the throne of our Redeemer
How refreshing it is!

Past sins forgiven!
Past troubles forgotten!
Past wounds healed!

What a wonderful blessing
To rule over mighty Angels
To enjoy an intimate fellowship
With white-robed Saints we love
What friendships we will have!

Our faith fulfilled
Our hopes realized
Our tears wiped away

What a wonderful blessing
To share in Christ's rule
To explore the boundless expanses
Of a glorious New Creation
Containing <u>no</u> death or decay

So unaccountable!
So incomprehensible!
So indescribable!

What a wonderful blessing
To have <u>no strife or trouble</u>
And to enjoy complete rest within ourselves
We have received that peace which enables us
To love our God with our whole being

We long to convey our pleasure
We long to convey our joy
We long to convey our ecstasy
When finally, we see Jesus face-to-face!

POSTSCRIPT: GUARD YOUR HEART

Pay attention! Give heed! Accept this final challenge!

If you fill your heart
With evil
Will not evil result?

If you fill your heart
With lies
Will not lies result?

If you fill your heart
With hatred
Will not hatred result?

If you fill your heart
With trivia
Will not trivia result?

If you fill your heart
With truth
Will not truth result?

If you fill your heart
With goodness
Will not goodness result?

If you fill your heart
With love
Will not love result?

As we part my friend
Let me exhort you
To <u>guard your heart</u>
Build fortifications around it
Protect it with plates of iron
Encase it in concrete
Leave no space for the enemy to enter

Beware of its weaknesses
And its tendency toward deception
Note how fickle and proud it can be

So …

Take care to feed your heart
With the Word of life
(The Holy Scriptures)
Let Jesus Christ fill it
And allow His spirit
To provide enlightenment where needed

Draw strength
From the bread and wine
He kindly offers.

In these perilous times
Of fire, flood and disease
<u>Guard your heart</u>
I repeat <u>GUARD YOUR HEART</u>
Avoid being fearful
Give no space to panic

Instead …

Pray for endurance, wisdom and guidance
Do all this
And you will find that your heart
Will become a reliable guide
Leading you into ways
That are right, peaceful and just

End Notes

Dates following the title show when each piece was first drafted.

All Praise: Friday, 28th January 2011 whilst scanning *'Hymns, Ancient and Modern'*

Behold: Monday, 11th September 2006 whilst seated on a large grey rock near the ridge line of a certain moor. It expresses the need to perceive God's providence in everything.

Come – Go In: Monday, 8th February 1988.

Elohim: Friday, 9th October 2009

Families: Wednesday, 13th September 1989. It expresses God's concern over every aspect of a healthy family life where there are no complicating factors such as disability or genetic disease. A reader may object to the optimistic tone of this piece by asking, *'What about the terrible cases of child abuse which take place in society?'* To some extent, this question may be answered in that God, (through the provision of natural resources and healthy social structures) has given everything needed for the successful rearing of children. However, Man, in all his sinfulness, has chosen to corrupt these things – thus spoiling the pre-determined environment. In Matthew 18:6-7 the Lord gave the severest possible warning against those who would stumble *'the little ones.'*

How Great: Sunday, 30th January 2005. Its theme is the need to receive the Holy Spirit in order to better understand and use scripture properly.

In the Stillness: Tuesday, 21st June 1988 whilst beginning a prayer retreat. It highlights the peaceful stillness which lies in the heart of God.

It Bestows: Friday, 11th October 2018

Life and Death: Saturday, 16th January 2010

My Heart: Friday, 23rd September 1988, when experiencing a revelation of divine love. It shows that God alone can give us a deep love for Himself and for others. This was the period when I was beginning to venture out into a church teaching ministry and needed a great deal of personal encouragement. The word *'burst'* is used here because (during this revelation of divine love) I personally felt a tremendous power of love burst outwards from me as if it were a volcanic geyser. (Performers may replace the word *'burst'* with *'is filled.'*)

Presence: Tuesday, 21st September 2004. Its theme is the Lord's Omnipresence – both inside and outside the present created order.
Rejoice: Sunday, 15th July 1984. Originally, it was an exhortation shared with a church congregation. It stresses how the love of God produces joy.
The Beauty of the Lord: Friday, 13th November 2009
The God of Holy Love: Tuesday, 27th January 2009
Trinity: Written sometime in early 1985 to highlight the need to adore all members of the Trinity in one's prayer life. (It had been used for private devotions since 1981.)
Triune Worship: Saturday, 19th June 2004. Written in the Chapel of a certain hospital. Its theme is the need to worship the Trinity in a creative way.
Wonderful Blessing: Thursday, 15th April 2019. Performers may encourage audience participation in the italicized parts.

Postscript: Guard Your Heart: Written on Tuesday, 25th February 2020. This was during a period consisting of many disasters including: -
- Uncontrolled bush fires in Australia
- Severe storms and flooding in the British Isles
- A global pandemic of the Coronavirus
- A major financial and economic downturn

The Coronavirus (known as COVID 19) originated in Wuhan, China during the previous December. From there it quickly spread across much of the world. By March, there was panic buying of sanitary products like toilet rolls in the United Kingdom. This left rows of empty shelves. Thankfully, my wife and I were already well stocked with that product! We did though notice that railway stations and other normally crowded places were very quiet. Towards the end of March, we were, like most of the rest of the UK population in self-isolation. Daily life had come to a standstill. It was all very strange.

SELECTIVE BIBLIOGRAPHY

Booklist

Barton Laurence (2001) *Crisis in Organizations II* South-Western College Publishing ISBN:0-324-02429-0

Hardman Isabel (2019) *Why We Get the Wrong Politicians* Atlantic Books ISBN: 978-1-78239-973-5

Lewis Staples Clive (1945) *The Great Divorce* Geoffrey Bles

Martel Frederic (2019) *In the Closet of the Vatican: Power, Homosexuality, Hypocrisy* Bloomsbury Continuum ISBN: 978-1-4729-6614-8

Molesky Mark (2015) *This Gulf of Fire: The Destruction of Lisbon, or Apocalypse in the Age of Science and Reason* Knopf Publishing Group SBN: 978-0307267627

Unattributed (2000) *Harvard Business Review on Crisis Management* Harvard School Press ISBN: 1-57851-235-3

Wesley John Rev. (1889) *A Collection of Hymns for use of The People Called The Methodists: With a New Supplement* London: Wesleyan-Methodist Book Room

Media Sources

BBC Two (January 2020) *Exposed – The Church's Darkest Secret: The Sexual Wrongdoing of Bishop Peter Ball (1932-2019)* BBC2 Episode 1 Monday, 13.1.2020

BBC Two (January 2020) *Exposed – The Church's Darkest Secret: The Sexual Wrongdoing of Bishop Peter Ball (1932-2019)* BBC2 Episode 2 Tuesday, 14.1.2020

OTHER TITLES BY THE AUTHOR

Notice

For information on the ordering and pricing of these titles please visit
http://stores.lulu.com/rebuildchristianity or
http://stores.lulu.com/store.php?fAcctID=976144

Soft cover versions of these titles should be available through Amazon and other International Distributors.

In the event of any difficulty with these *'links'* please search using the *'Book Title' and* the name *'Raymond Creed.'* Doing this should access a relevant site.

THE 52 ATTRIBUTES OF GOD

'The 52 Attributes of God' explores God's unique character. It uses ancient Jewish methods of bible interpretation ('Midrash') along with prayerful meditations, proverbial sayings and simple summaries. Each chapter combines both analytical with devotional material and readers are encouraged to progress at their own pace. 'The 52 Attributes of God' is readily accessible for both private and group use and employs a stimulating variety of questions to aid reflection and to encourage practical application. It shows how all 52 of the divine attributes were displayed during Christ's death and it helps rebuild Christianity by using 'Midrash' to provide a clearer picture of God's nature. Great care is taken to answer such questions as: -
1) Who is God?
2) What is He like?
3) How did He react to the death of His Son Jesus?
4) How does He react to the corruption found within much of today's Church?
5) To what extent can we become like God?

'The 52 Attributes of God' should prove particularly useful to religious ministers (of all denominational backgrounds), local church elders, Christian teachers, evangelists and theological students. The Messianic Jewish community and those wishing to delve deeper into theology would especially benefit. Any public or academic library with a theological section will find it a rich resource. It should also be of assistance to those confused or troubled by beguiling *'spiritualities'* which alluringly offer the chance to become divine.

This book ends by warning that those choosing to ignore the clear distinction between God and Man (by presuming they have a right to become mini gods) often end up behaving like devils. To purchase a download, hard or soft cover edition please visit:
http://stores.lulu.com/rebuildchristianity or
http://stores.lulu.com/store.php?fAcctID=976144
Soft cover editions may also be available through Amazon and other International Distributors.

FACING THE UNTHINKABLE

'Facing the Unthinkable' dramatically portrays the likely emotional and psychological reactions of a beleaguered number of Jewish people at the very point when they turn to their true Messiah. Their state of near-total despair will suddenly change to one of exuberant joy. Following their recognition and acceptance of the Messiah all of the bible prophecies concerning the restoration of Israel will begin to be fulfilled.

'Facing the Unthinkable' provides hope for the Messianic Jewish Community and for those Christians with a genuine interest in the Jewish people. It helps rebuild Christianity by emphasising its links to both Israel and Judaism.

Great care is taken to address the following questions: -
1) How will the Jewish people come to believe in their true Messiah?
2) How will they react when they encounter Him?
3) How will the world react to this unexpected development?

This book breaks new ground in its creative expression of the spiritual and psychological aspects likely to be experienced when the true Messiah is recognised. It's assumed that both the nation of Israel and the whole of humanity itself will be on the brink of annihilation before this unique event happens. God will have allowed much suffering to have taken place to show man's abject failure in his attempt to create a New World Order. The promise of a better and fairer world will have been cruelly exposed and falsified.

'Facing the Unthinkable' is an invaluable resource for those engaged in any form of Jewish work or who have a sympathetic interest in the State of Israel. It may be regarded as an independent work or as a successor volume to 'The Leeds Liturgy.' To purchase a download, hard or soft cover edition please visit: -
http://stores.lulu.com/rebuildchristianity or
http://stores.lulu.com/store.php?fAcctID=976144
Soft cover editions may also be available through Amazon and other International Distributors.

THE LEEDS LITURGY

'The Leeds Liturgy' encourages Christians to worship God *"in spirit and in truth"* (John 4:24). In terms of doctrine, it aspires to be the truest and most accurate book outside of scripture. Its pages contain *'The Leeds Creed'* which is the most comprehensive creedal *'Statement of Faith'* in Christianity to date, (Acts 20:27). This *'statement'* integrates bible-based insights from every Christian Tradition and provides a comprehensive summary of those doctrines needed for salvation and for effective Christian living. Also included are revised versions of the Apostles, Nicene and Athanasian Creeds.

'The Leeds Liturgy' aims to: -
1) Provide a legacy of truth for present and future believers
2) Testify to the one true Gospel that *"Jesus Christ came into the world to save sinners,"* (I Timothy 1:15b)
3) Portray doctrine in a fresh, interactive and understandable way
4) Promote an exuberant style of worship
5) Declare the *whole counsel [full teaching] of God* to a Church that currently seems to value everything else but the teaching of Scripture
6) Enable believers (largely due to its provision of sound doctrinal teaching) to better withstand persecution and hardship
7) Bring Jew and Gentile together in joint worship of the one true God of Israel
8) Nurture the community life of Messianic Jewish and Christian groups
9) Offer a distinctive way of presenting timeless truths to a sinful world
10) Enable believers to interact with bible teaching (either individually or in a group setting)

'The Leeds Liturgy' proclaims the Gospel by pointing to Christ as the only means whereby eternal life is received. His full deity and full humanity are equally emphasised – as is the Trinitarian relationship between Himself, His Father and the Holy Spirit. Christians are encouraged to relate to These Persons through the material provided in this resource. It

attempts to be a vehicle with the innate capacity to be used by the Holy Spirit, who eagerly wants to lead Christians into all truth, (John 16:13a). It highlights the fact that, in order to place our faith in God, we must first of all lose faith in ourselves.

'The Leeds Liturgy' closes with two articles exploring the biblical roots of Liturgies and Creeds. These could be of particular interest to students working in the field of liturgical studies. Its successor volume, 'Facing the Unthinkable' provides a dramatic anticipation of how Israel will recognize the true messiah during a period of great affliction. To purchase a download, hard or soft cover edition please visit: -
http://stores.lulu.com/rebuildchristianity or
http://stores.lulu.com/store.php?fAcctID=976144
Soft cover versions may also be available through Amazon and other International Distributors.

THE PHANTOM CONFLICT

'The Phantom Conflict' endeavours to rebuild Christianity by showing how a balanced emphasis between divine holiness and divine love is a necessary prerequisite for healthy Christian living. The problem of Christian idolatry is also tackled.

Great care is taken to address the following questions: -
1) How does divine holiness relate to divine love?
2) How is it possible to avoid incorrect views of God?
3) How is it possible to avoid idolatry?

'The Phantom Conflict,' assumes that correct ideas of God are a vital precondition to spiritual fruitfulness. It argues that to exaggerate divine holiness at the expense of divine love (or vice-versa) produces a warped and ineffective version of Christianity. At one extreme it becomes a religion of fear and at the other a religion of flippancy. Both deviations harm their adherents and discredit the gospel.

This book should prove particularly useful to religious ministers (of all denominational backgrounds), local church elders, Christian teachers, evangelists and theological students. The Messianic Jewish community and those wishing to delve deeper into theology would also benefit.

'The Phantom Conflict' serves as a practical and interactive teaching tool, being divided into easily accessible sections, all undergirded by ancient Jewish methods of bible interpretation (*'Midrash'*). It may be regarded as an independent work or as a successor volume to *'The 52 Attributes of God.'*

To purchase a download, hard or soft cover edition please visit: -
http://stores.lulu.com/rebuildchristianity or
http://stores.lulu.com/store.php?fAcctID=976144
Soft cover editions may also be available through Amazon and other International Distributors.

NOTES

www.ingramcontent.com/pod-product-compliance
Lightning Source LLC
Chambersburg PA
CBHW071648090426
42738CB00009B/1454